HIS:

Your bachelor party is your last chance to celebrate the freedom and perks enjoyed by single males everywhere. For instance, paying surgically altered women to take off their clothes. Or drinking until you throw up on yourself.

HERS:

You are not his hangover nurse. The "in sickness and in health" deal doesn't go into effect until your wedding day, and you don't deserve to watch him mope around in misery the day after his bachelor party.

For many couples, the wedding is the first chance to negotiate big issues together—not to mention a few million little issues, from selecting postage stamps to agreeing on party favors. Mutual understanding is the key to finding easy, stress-free solutions. Now, with short alternating chapters that bring you both "his" and "her" points of view, you'll find the kind of wise, witty advice and emotional support you need as you deal with . . .

MONEY: Want to see a grown father of the bride cry?

MUSIC: Band, DJ, or Uncle Larry the guitorganist?

COLD FEET: You're absolutely 100 percent, no-doubt-about-it sure. So why are you so scared?

THE GIFT REGISTRY: What are you planning to do, exactly, with sixteen parfait glasses?

THE REHEARSAL DINNER: Surviving the joining of two families in a room full of forks.

PLUS: THE DRESS, THE VOWS, THE PHOTOS, THE PARENTS, THE THANK-YOUS, and all the other obstacles on your road to matrimonial bliss!

Surviving Your WEDDING

A HIS AND HER GUIDE

Wendy and David Hubbert

B
BERKLEY BOOKS, NEW YORK

SURVIVING YOUR WEDDING: A HIS AND HER GUIDE

A Berkley Book / published by arrangement with
the authors

PRINTING HISTORY
Berkley trade paperback edition / January 2000

The Penguin Putnam Inc. World Wide Web site address is
http://www.penguinputnam.com

ISBN: 0-425-17270-8

BERKLEY®
Berkley Books are published by The Berkley Publishing Group,
a division of Penguin Putnam Inc., 375 Hudson Street, New York, New York 10014.
BERKLEY and the "B" design
are trademarks belonging to Penguin Putnam Inc.

PRINTED IN THE UNITED STATES OF AMERICA

10 9 8 7 6 5 4 3 2

Contents

ARRANGEMENTS

BRIDE VS. GROOM

THE EVENT

THE AFTERMATH

Acknowledgments

LIKE weddings themselves, a book about weddings can only be coaxed into existence through the combined efforts of many people. We owe our gratitude to the many recently married and engaged couples who freely gave us their stories and advice, and to our friends, relatives, and colleagues whose weddings we were fortunate enough to attend, enjoy, and take notes on.

We offer our deep appreciation to Angela Miller and Selene Ahn, who have guided us well through two books, and to the Berkley team, including editor Denise Silvestro.

Finally, the warmest of thanks go to our families, who forgave us for not visiting during many months of writing and who helped us happily survive our own wedding.

Introduction

Six years ago, we set out to throw ourselves the perfect wedding. We expected nothing less for the most important day of our lives: perfect vows, a perfect reception, a perfect honeymoon. Perfect, perfect, perfect. We had attended enough weddings to know what we liked and disliked, so we were confident we could take our ceremony by the reins and guide it straight into the annals of matrimonial history. Our guests would weep with joy at the beautiful spectacle unfolding before them, laughing when they were supposed to laugh, crying when they were supposed to cry, returning to their homes with a smile in their hearts and one thought in their heads: "Now *that* was a perfect wedding!"

Then we looked at our budget. The word "perfect" never came up in conversation again.

In fact, when we think back on our wedding, and the year of planning that preceded it, the embarrassing *im*perfections are among our favorite memories: ridiculous tantrums over the guest list; wedding dresses fitted, purchased, returned, refitted, returned, and finally rented; miscues during the ceremony; and our triumphant march to the middle of the dance floor—where we completely forgot four months of rhumba lessons.

We're not unique. Every married couple will tell you the funniest three stories about their wedding before they get to the teary-eyed father-daughter dance. Of course, these stories only seem humorous after the fact. In the heat of nuptial planning and its aftermath they appear deadly serious. Why? Because history tells us that a wedding is an *enormous* deal—a rite of passage, a transfer of wealth, a family showcase, a status symbol, a crippling expense, and an opulent party all wrapped into one massive ceremony.

On top of that, planning your wedding is like being married in microcosm. In the next year or so, you'll learn many of the skills essential to your survival as husband and wife, such as financial management, mutual decision making, getting along with each others' parents, handling disagreements, and solving problems. You may face many of these issues for the first time in your lives, and if you have any memories of learning to walk, read, drive, or calculate the radius of a circle, you know how hard it can be to comprehend something new.

In the midst of this tough learning curve and all this seriousness, while you're daydreaming of a wedding that is the ultimate expression of undying love, remember to leave room for Uncle Ralph to dance on a table with the bride's veil on his head. It may be disheartening to imagine that you'll spend hundreds of hours, thousands of dollars, and millions of brain cells on an event that will be fondly remembered by attendees as the wedding where Ralph went nuts. But by eliminating "perfect" from your vocabulary and putting your wedding into a more realistic perspective, we hope this survival guide makes the planning and execution of "the most important day of your life" a little less stressful, a lot more fun, and not quite so, well... important.

What you're reading is not a wedding planner, nor is it as linear and chronological as a step-by-step, day-by-day outline for achieving the wedding of your dreams. Some couples begin the planning process by dealing with the guest list, others go right for the honeymoon; some have problems with parents; and others have problems with friends. Still others have no problems with people at all, it's color schemes and buffet tables that give them pause.

No need to worry, it's all covered in these pages, right down to intangible issues you may not have imagined would occur, like power struggles, unavoidable crises, and stage fright.

Just as there is no right way to plan a wedding, there isn't a preferred way to read this book. If the cake is what's on your mind today, skip to that chapter now for some interesting stories borrowed from real couples and some valuable cake-cutting advice. You'll notice that "The Cake," like every chapter, has both a "His" and a "Her" side of the story. These provide the often complementary, sometimes wildly off-kilter views of the two most important people at any wedding: the bride and the groom.

Through countless conversations with newlyweds and engaged couples, we've found that, quite often in wedding planning, the male perspective is ignored from the moment "girlfriend" becomes "fiancée." But since marriage itself is a fifty-fifty deal, your wedding should be no different. On issues heretofore relegated to the realm of the female, a man's point of view can be useful and insightful—or at the very least, hilarious. And you may be surprised to hear what brides have to say about the bachelor party, the grooms-men's gifts, or the bathing habits of the best man.

The "His and Her" format isn't meant to be read as "Him against Her." On the contrary, our goal is to help you work better *together* through a proper understanding of each others' unique needs and opinions. Although the "His" chapters are addressed to the groom and "Hers" to the bride, we encourage you both to read both sides of each issue, then talk to each other about it. You may be able to snip off a few problems before they blossom into all-out disasters. And you'll constantly reinforce the most vital idea of all— that no matter what happens, you're in this together, now and for as long you both shall live.

One friendly bit of advice before you read on: You're not creating the space program or eliminating world hunger. You're throwing a wedding. While getting married may be the most important thing you'll do in the next few years, it shouldn't consume your every waking moment. At least once a week, try to share a meal together with your fiancé and talk about something *other* than your wedding plans. Do little romantic things to remind yourselves that this whole production is a celebration of how much you love each other. As the ceremony draws near, take a long weekend away, and leave the guest lists, seating charts, and song selections behind.

In short, remember to enjoy yourselves. If all goes well, your wedding will be a once-in-a-lifetime event, so savor every moment, both the disastrous and the transcendent. We hope you find this guide helpful in navigating the ups and downs of your big day, and we wish for you a truly wonderful, enjoyable—anything but "perfect"—wedding experience.

The Key Elements

· Hers ·

PLACE, DATE, AND TIME

YOU'VE been engaged for all of five minutes, and you call your best friend to relate the good news. But instead of joyously making plans for dress shopping and bachelorette partying, your friend demands, "When is it? And where?" You admit you've planned neither of the above, and your friend squawks, "*What?* Do you have any idea how quickly places get booked these days?" You hang up the phone in tears, convinced you'll be having your reception at the local Chuck E. Cheese's. Brides with more on the ball than you have booked every other possible site through 2010.

Don't panic! Your friend may have your best interests at heart, but she's exaggerating a teensy bit. Most places don't book up *quite* that quickly, and the good news about planning a wedding is, once you've nailed down the time and place, you can (almost) relax a little. The challenge, though, is that, in order to pick a time or place, you have to make some decisions about the *kind* of wedding you want. While you'd much rather be celebrating the fact that you're going to be married, necessity dictates that you and your fiancé start talking seriously about the manner in which you'd like to do so.

Close your eyes and picture yourself getting married. What kind of wedding do you see yourself having? Are your guests dressed formally or casually? Is it morning, afternoon, or nighttime? Are you indoors or outdoors? Here are some other things to consider:

- Large or small

- Budget or lavish

- Ceremony and reception in same place or separate

- Modern or traditional

- Religious or secular

- Winter, spring, summer, or fall

- Formal or casual

- Local or distant

Try to agree upon a shared vision with your fiancé. Your goal is to be able to say with certainty that you both see yourselves, for example, getting married outside among autumn leaves, followed by a casual meal with your closest friends and family members. This vision gives you a great place to start your planning.

Common sense, your budget, and the needs of your guests will help you narrow things down even more. If the majority of your guests will have to travel a good distance to your wedding, holding it on a Sunday evening before a normal workday may not be a good idea, unless you want to see a mass exodus immediately after dinner. You can make it easier on guests who need to travel by having the ceremony and reception in one place, so they don't have to arrange transportation or fumble around in unfamiliar territory. If you're on a budget, you'll want to stay away from a black-tie Saturday evening event. That's prime real estate in the wedding world, and you'll be charged accordingly by reception hall managers. Watch out for freak holidays, too. If the

As you're homing in on the right place, date, and time for your wedding, you may end up brainstorming quirky ideas for the *style* of your ceremony and reception. Some you'll find are great and some are just plain silly. Here's a guide to good and bad style ideas that can help set you straight:

Good Idea: A country theme, with horse-drawn hayrides, apple cider, and a roaring fire in a big stone hearth.

Bad Idea: Outhouses or Port-O-Potties. Some things stop being quaint when your guests try to navigate them in high heels.

Good Idea: A taste of the sea: maybe a wedding on the beach, or a reception hall transformed into a seaside cabana, complete with a reggae band.

Bad Idea: A boat trip. Not everyone enjoys sailing on the open water, and guests are supposed to feel sick the day *after* a great wedding, not the day *of.*

Good Idea: Have your wedding at a local landmark so guests can use free time to wander around and get a sense of the area's history.

Bad Idea: Having your wedding somewhere *too* distracting, like an amusement park. There may be no one around to see you say "I do."

Good Idea: Ethnic food that reflects your heritage or a style of cooking that you particularly enjoy.

Bad Idea: Serving *only* that ethnic food. Uncle Leon may raise a ruckus if his only choice for dinner is tekka maki rolls.

reception hall of your dreams is in the green bean capital of the world, you're clearly not going to be able to reserve that place on National Green Bean Day.

The biggest regret I've heard from newlyweds is that they let tradition dictate their whole wedding, rather than planning a place, time, and style that truly reflect their personalities. There's no need to have candlelit tables, champagne, and duck à l'orange when you really want to host a barbecue for fifty of your closest friends. One bride we spoke with had her ceremony and reception on Halloween in an S&M-themed bar. Her mother's only wish was to see her daughter wed in a traditional princess dress, so the bride wore a flowery lace, pearl, and satin number—jet black. She may not have pleased everyone, but she certainly made herself happy.

Of course, a little compromise may be necessary when the family members footing the bill start to demand a certain kind of wedding. Ann-Marie wanted a casual affair rather than a sit-down dinner, but her grandmother (who was chipping in several thousand dollars) objected, saying, "You can't spend my money to have a pizza party." Ann-Marie ultimately planned a formal wedding with some casual touches. The most important thing for her was to keep the family peace: "A wedding is a few hours," she decided. "A family is forever."

· His ·

PLACE, DATE, AND TIME

So you finally popped the question. Congratulations! Now begins the most memorable, irritating, decision-packed year of your life. What are the first few of the many decisions to come? For most people, those are where and when to have the wedding.

Fortunately, the planet on which your wedding will be held is a foregone conclusion (believe me, there would be an argument over it if it wasn't), but some couples still have to start with "Which continent?" before they get to "Which region, state, and city?" Many weddings are held somewhere near the bride's parents. But maybe your fiancée has no special attachment to her childhood home, or perhaps neither of you have any special attachment to her parents. In that case, locations that have romantic meaning to you as a couple make great wedding choices. Try the place where you first met. Or where you first kissed. Or wherever you were when you first realized that this woman was destined to be your lifelong soulmate. Hopefully it wasn't Antarctica.

Once you nail down the area, it's time to start looking for a building that will hold you and up to five hundred of your closest friends. You need to decide on an approximate number of expected guests before you begin looking. Obviously, if your wedding is large you can't book a place that's too cozy, but the opposite is true as well. If you're planning an intimate wedding, you want a room that's small enough to look full when your guests arrive, unless you have some sort of minimalist theme going. You should have some idea of when you want to get married; it's best to narrow it down to a particular month but not necessarily a date. Flexibility is important at this stage, because the place you want may not be available on the exact day you want it.

Not to put too much pressure on you, but the locations of your ceremony and reception are the most important wedding decisions you'll make. When you attend a wedding as a guest, what do you remember most? The place. In fact, ten years later, the place may be the *only* thing you remember about someone else's wedding. That's an important fact to keep in mind when you're faced with a myriad of grueling smaller decisions during the planning process. Remember to ask yourself, and your fiancée, "Will the guests really remember that the pink chryflanthigolds clashed with the orange jack-in-the whatsits?"

Since location is so important, it's best to plan it out thoroughly. Do you want the ceremony in a church or synagogue and the reception somewhere else? Do you want it all in one place as long as it's outside? If you do go with an outside wedding, do you have an inside option or a tent if it rains? Will your guests have interesting places to wander throughout the evening or will they be stuck in the same room all night?

If the choice of location were always left to men, more weddings would be held on the pitcher's mound at Yankee Stadium or underwater in the Bahamas wearing a rubber top hat and tails. This fits our definition of a cool wedding. If this is your second or third time walking down the aisle, it may make sense to add "cool" to your list of matrimonial requirements, but most first-time brides prefer a standard beautiful wedding with friends and flowers and crying and romance. Thus parachutes, while definitely cool, will probably not figure into your wedding plans.

That doesn't mean you can't be creative with location. Wendy and I found an eighteenth-century church that had been converted to a university lecture hall, with the most interesting historical elements left in place. It had a pipe organ, basement catacombs with ancient bones on display, and, outside, a graveyard complete with the last resting place of Edgar Allen Poe. Sound morbid? The guests loved it. During lulls in the reception, many stepped outside hoping for a chance glimpse of the Raven, then ducked back in for the cutting of the cake. There are bound to be equally interesting places in your chosen area.

For guys, it can be all too tempting to jump at the first place that seems acceptable, falls in your price range, and is available when you want it to be. Spending weekend after weekend getting the old sales pitch from one reception hall manager after another isn't our idea of fun. But an exhaustive search now will yield the greatest satisfaction on your wedding day, when you, your family, and your guests all confirm that you found a great place. Besides, nothing is more painful than locking in your wedding location, then stumbling onto a far better place a month before the ceremony.

There are dozens of resources for wedding venues. Try the phone book under "weddings" or "receptions," and follow up with an Internet search. Call your local chamber of commerce and ask for a list of interesting wedding spots, especially historical sites. Ask your friends, your parents, and your parents' friends for the locations of the best weddings they've attended. Compile a list of possibles and go see them one by one.

Where your wedding will be often dictates when it will be. Popular locations book well in advance, so you may find the perfect place is only available on a Tuesday night three years from now. That's why it's important to make this decision early in the process. Keep in mind that Sunday nights are generally easier to get than Saturday nights, and holiday weekends are tougher than regular weekends. If you're lucky enough to be sure of the one place where the two of you always wanted to be married, then the only question mark is when. Just book that place now, because everything else you do, and all the other topics in this book, will hinge on where you decide to tie the knot.

· *Hers* ·

FOOD

NEXT to location, the food is the most important element of your reception. Caterers can dish it up hot or cold, fresh or wilted, on a plate with garnish or slopped in a bowl. On a whim, they can choose to accommodate your diabetic aunt, vegetarian sister-in-law, and sixteen nieces and nephews in high chairs, or they can make your life a living hell. Make no mistake, with catered food you don't get what you pay for, you get what they want to give you. The caterer is God, as far as you're concerned, and you'd better choose your religion carefully.

Before you hire a caterer, it's a good idea to meet with several candidates, preferably in their own kitchens. You're not just checking out the taste of their food, you're seeing how they work and what their priorities are. Are they big on presentation, making sure the food will look beautiful when it hits the table? Or are they primarily concerned with ensuring that everyone gets a hot plate of something fast? Are they open to special requests, or are you so lucky to have them working for you that you'd better warn vegetarians to bring a sack lunch? Does the wait staff have relevant experience, or will your guests be served by temps from FelonFinders?

When you meet with prospective caterers, you'll be tempted to focus on food choices and costs. But remember, you'll be working intimately for several months with these people, especially your key contact person, so take note of how she treats you and how comfortable you feel with her. If her attitude irritates you at this initial meeting, it probably won't get any better.

Many caterers have been immersed for so long in the wedding world that they speak a special caterer-language. You may on occasion find yourself without the slightest clue of what they're talking about. In order to give you cost estimates, the caterer will ask things like how many passed hors d'oeuvres you want, and whether you want a buffet with or without stations versus a sit-down meal. Whoa, Nelly! What's a passed hors d'oeuvre? What are stations? "I just want *food*," you scream inside your head. "Tell me how much you're charging me for *food!*"

Worse still, in order to figure out which food to serve and how much it's going to cost, caterers will ask you to make all kinds of decisions that link up with all kinds of other decisions about things you haven't even begun to think about yet. So you're forced to think in the hypothetical, which is intensely frustrating, and every question you're asked leads to a catch-22. "I can't possibly tell you what kind of food I want to serve so that you can give me an estimate because the reception hall hasn't yet told me if I can have the six P.M. Saturday slot or if I'm stuck with ten A.M. Sunday and I can't decide whether to invite four hundred guests or whether I'm just going to elope."

Caterers will always make you feel as though your budget is totally inadequate. They'll never, ever say, "Fifty dollars a head? Fantastic! We'll do x, y, and z, and you'll be thrilled." Instead, you'll hear: *Sigh.* "Well, fifty dollars is right at the cutoff point. If you could go any higher, we could do the all-truffle meal and that would be really special. But if fifty dollars is your absolute limit, we'll do the best we can. Don't worry—food isn't the most important thing about your wedding." The caterer's goal is to push you to stretch a little further, and make you feel as if whatever you can afford is just not going to be good enough for your guests. This is a carefully premeditated distraction technique to keep you from wondering why a piece of fish with a side of noodles costs twenty-seven dollars.

It would be easier to ignore caterer-guilt if you hadn't been on the other end of so many weddings, listening as a guest, to all those evil conversations about the food. "Is this chicken—or rubber?" "Pigs-in-a-blanket! I haven't had these since my trailer days." "Is this for eating or for show?" "Chipped beef on toast! It's just like summer camp!" "Let's get Mikey. He'll eat any-thing."

You don't want this to happen at your wedding, so you'll allow yourself to be talked into adding all kinds of useless extras. I suspect that caterers follow the automobile dealer school of management: "Now, I'd have to check with the boss, because we normally don't do this kind of thing, but I think if you just spend three dollars more per plate, we can throw in an arugula and orange blossom garnish that will make people think you're paying at least a hundred a head."

As if you're not squeezed enough between your budget, your caterer's "vision," and your own great expectations, at a certain point your guests will weigh in with special requests. Vegetarians are fairly easy to accommodate, but some guests equate the wedding meal with dining out in a fine restau-rant. The catch is, you have to take their orders waaaay in advance. Nicky from St. Louis is on a salt-restricted diet; Bobby from upstate just had his cho-lesterol checked and must have a low-fat meal. No, he can't simply scrape the sauce off. One couple had to make the entire reception kosher, because of one kosher cousin.

The various demands of guests can make it difficult to be truly creative with your menu selections. But that's probably a blessing in disguise. You may be wild about the caterer's proposal of slow-roasted platypus in a tar-ragon, rose petal, and saffron demi-glace with pecan-crusted hearts of palm and persimmon-spice-drenched sweetbreads, but your guests will be happy if they just get a meal they can identify.

· His ·

FOOD

AAAAH, now here's something you can really get worked up about—food. Nobody ever accused you of being late for a good meal, so if any decision requires your full attention, it's this one. But before you can decide on a menu, you have to go shopping for a caterer, and that's not always as easy as flipping open the Yellow Pages to "C."

Many hotels and wedding reception halls require that you use an in-house caterer. This has a number of advantages. Since the caterer has worked there before, he or she knows the kitchen and the dining room. You're paying one vendor for two services, so you should be able to save some money. Unfortunately, you may not get the most inspired (or even well-cooked) meal, simply because the in-house caterer figures you're stuck with him. And what are you going to do if you're unhappy with the food? Send it back? On your wedding day? The caterer isn't exactly worried about ensuring your repeat business.

If your reception hall allows you to shop around for caterers, I recommend you make the effort. And don't just go for the biggest name in town because he or she's the easiest to reach. Think of McDonald's, with over a

Decoding the Caterer's Menu

Menus are like little advertisements for food, and, as such, they employ exaggerated descriptions and overblown gourmet embellishments to get your tastebuds humming. Here's a quick lesson in wedding-caterer-speak.

What the menu says	What you get
Tender baby asparagus spears in a piquant Hollandaise sauce	Limp green Link'n Logs drenched in Velveeta.
Mixed baby greens tossed with raspberry walnut vinaigrette	Rabbit food in stinky oil
Medallions of chicken fanned over a bed of spinach risotto	Six McNuggets on a pile of green Rice-A-Roni
Beef Wellington with skillet-seared potato pancakes	Hamburger Helper and a side of hash browns
Salmon paté and English biscuits	Nine Lives Seafood Feast and saltines

billion served and a franchise on every street corner. Exactly how much loving care goes into the preparation and presentation of your Quarter Pounder with Cheese? The diner on the opposite corner serves far fewer customers, but needs each one of those customers to survive. For an extra dollar or two, they make an effort to give you a better meal. It's the same with caterers. The most attentive and creative catering companies are often the smallest, the ones that host fewer than two or three weddings a month. While they may be a little more expensive per plate, the extra effort they make will be apparent on the happy faces of your guests.

In the end, your guests are the only factors to consider in choosing your caterer, because there's no way you're going to have time to eat at your own reception. Nope, you've got to personally greet each and every guest, and the only time you'll have to do that is during the meal. So all those hours you spend poring over menus, agonizing over the choice between filet mignon and coconut-encrusted snapper, drooling over the artichoke appetizer, and taste-testing the creamy peppercorn salad dressing, will be only a prelude to the official meal of happy newlyweds everywhere: cold dinner rolls and mini-bar vodka.

Keep in mind, you're not committed to serving dinner at your wedding. If you're getting married early in the day, it's perfectly acceptable to serve lunch or brunch. Whatever meal you plan to provide, encourage your caterer to be creative. Flower petal salads, palate-cleansing sherbet between courses, and chocolates at every place setting are the kind of little touches that make a meal great. And that's important, because the best way to your wedding guests' hearts is through lots of satisfying food. That, and a four-station martini bar.

Hers

Music

FOR the guests at your wedding, good music can mean the difference between stampeding for the door after you cut the cake, and needing a crowbar to create more room on the dance floor. I've seen Sunday ten A.M. weddings turn into raucous parties, and six P.M. Saturday night receptions end after two hours, depending on the strength or weakness of the music. So it's important to decide upon the mood you want to create, and work hard to provide the appropriate musical score right from the start.

First, you'll need accompaniment for the ceremony. Many houses of worship come with resident organists who will work your wedding for a small fee. Or your priest, pastor, rabbi, or cantor, having officiated dozens of weddings, may be able to recommend a string quartet that's fluent in "The Wedding March." These musicians will offer you the usual options for background music while the guests are being seated, music for the wedding party, your big entrance, your big exit, and various hymns or traditional songs. If you want something less traditional, the best musicians will be able to play more unusual but equally appropriate pieces that will make your wedding stand out from the crowd. But if you're sticking with the classics, I recommend you don't break the bank on ceremony accompaniment. There's no need to book the New York Philharmonic when Aunt Gertrude can play a perfectly passable "Ode to Joy" on the piano.

The reception is more complicated. If you're like most brides, your guest list will include people of all ages and tastes. It's next to impossible to arrange for music that will please your ninety-three-year-old grandmother, your parents' bosses, your club-hopping friends from work, *and* your head-banging little brother. It's best to resign yourself early to the fact that you can't expect every one of your guests to be happy at all times. A good band or DJ will be able to gauge the mood of the crowd and change his style from formal to casual at key points, after dinner for instance, or when the older people leave to catch reruns of *Murder, She Wrote.*

Because the music played at weddings tends to be full of the same old standards, a bride with unusual taste may find it a challenge to provide the unexpected. Sharon, being a musician herself, was very particular about the music at her wedding. For the reception, she compiled a list of seventy-five possible songs the DJ could play, and nothing else. Since many of her choices weren't on the average wedding/bar mitzvah/retirement home set list, she had a tough time finding a DJ with all, or even most, of her music in his collection. To make things tougher still, her wedding was to be held in her hometown, five hundred miles away from where she was currently living, so all these arrangements had to be made long-distance. Just try getting a good feel for how a DJ will perform from a five-minute phone interview!

So did all the extra effort pay off? Did Sharon's guests appreciate the fruits of her iron-fisted musical labor? For those who were fellow musicians, the answer was a resounding yes. But for the average crowd, exerting too much control over any aspect of your wedding, especially the music, is bound to backfire. Consider the story of LeeAnn, who was so concerned her friends would ridicule her for hiring a wacky DJ that she asked him to tone his act way down. He went 180 degrees away from his usual persona, providing exactly what LeeAnn asked for—a reserved, sophisticated host playing elegant, refined music. Afterward, LeeAnn admitted that her wedding might not have been as much fun as it could have, all because she was too concerned about what her friends would think.

As much as you want the music on your wedding day to reflect your personality, it's not your job to dictate the volume and tone of every note. Your wedding and reception will sound just fine if you follow one simple rule of thumb: Hire solid professionals or a band with good credentials and allow them to do what they do best.

· *His* ·

Music

ALMOST every stage of the wedding ceremony and reception is marked by musical cues that tell guests what to do. Guests stand when they hear "Here Comes the Bride," clap when they hear "The Recessional March," and when they hear "(Shake, Shake, Shake) Shake Your Booty," well, hopefully they do as they're told.

Behind every smooth-flowing wedding there is a great soundtrack. After your wedding is over, your guests may not remember the individual songs they heard, but they will judge the overall quality of the organist, band, DJ, or five-piece saxophone combo you hired. So it makes sense to put some serious effort into your choice of musical director. Just be warned that unless you hire a friend or relative to play your ceremony and reception, someone's going to have to pay the piper big bucks.

So open up your soon-to-be father-in-law's checkbook and gas up the car, because you want to find the best band in town and you have to see them in action. If you're lucky, you'll remember an amazing band that played at a friend's wedding and they'll be available on your wedding day. But if you're starting from scratch, there are two places you can sample the delights of this strange creation known as the Wedding Band, and both are equally weird.

The first is a wedding exhibit trade show or, as I like to call it, the Gong Show's Evil Spawn. Here, in the local convention center or high school gym, on a makeshift stage high above all the florist, photographer, and caterer booths, bands with names like Sax and Violins, Magical Journey, and We Could Have Been the Next Air Supply play their hearts out to a critical audience of trade show attendees, none of whom are in any mood to dance. In this sterile, artificial environment, you won't get a very clear picture of what each band is like at a real wedding, but you will hear how well they play. More importantly, you'll see how good a master of ceremonies the lead singer is, which will help you imagine what this person would be like announcing your first dance, emceeing the bouquet and garter tosses, and convincing your father to join in the Electric Slide. If he can get a rise out of a convention center crowd, he definitely has what it takes to work your wedding.

The other place to sample a band in action is at an actual wedding. No doubt about it, crashing someone else's wedding just to stand there and listen to the band is an awkward experience, but thankfully it's not an unusual one. Many bands will invite you to poke your head in when they play an upcoming event, and chances are, the couple getting married won't really mind as long as you refrain from lining your pockets with their cocktail weenies. Observing prospective bands at a wedding is a great way to get a true picture of how they work the crowd. Besides, you may even spot some fun party ideas to steal for your own reception.

Things to look for in a great wedding band include diverse set lists (each band should be able to provide you with one as part of their promotional package) with at least a few songs composed after 1979; a rapport with the crowd that isn't snotty, whiny, or desperate; clothing that's reasonably hole-, sequin-, and glitter-free; no evidence of toupees; and a genuine feeling that the band members are having fun.

Remember, growing up, most of these band members wanted to be Van Halen, or at least Harry Connick, Jr., and they all went through a period of bitterness and self-hatred once they realized that was never going to happen. The best bands to hire are the ones who are over it already. They accept that they were put on this earth to play weddings, bar mitzvahs, and fiftieth anniversary parties, not to pack stadiums, and that's okay. They'll earn a few extra bucks each weekend, and do the best darn job they can convincing the average Joe and Joanna to Bunny Hop, gamely trying to play requests, and scarfing down a free meal.

If you can't stand the thought of paying some glorified karaoke diva to belt out Mariah Carey at your wedding, you might be better off hiring a disc jockey willing to play a CD of Mariah's greatest hits. Some people frown on DJs, fretting that they're not classy enough for something as upscale as a wedding. Well, how classy is it when nobody under sixty is dancing to Tommy Dorsey favorites? Face it, a DJ will play anything you want, from Beethoven to the Buggles to "Rock Me Amadeus," and if you don't want a smoke machine, a strobe light, or the Chicken Dance to sully your high-class affair, then all you have to do tell the DJ ahead of time.

Remember, though, if you'll accept nothing less than a classy wedding, be sure to only invite classy guests. The DJ we hired for our wedding assured us that whenever a bride demands "No Chicken Dance!" at least ten of her guests will request it. Most times, we were told, the guests win out because their need to remember the wedding as "fun" outweighs the bride's hope that they'll remember the wedding as "classy."

·Hers·

FLOWERS

HERE it is, six years after my wedding, and still I catch myself bemoaning the choice of floral arrangements at my reception. Sure, it's ancient history, and sure, I've moved on. But if I'd only known then what I know now, everything really would have been perfect....

Sorry. I had to give myself a sharp slap on the wrist. As we know, "perfect" is a four-letter word as far as planning your wedding is concerned. But at least I can make myself feel better by offering some advice that will help you make wiser floral choices than I did.

With our florist, as with our photographer and our caterer, Dave and I had to make a decision between hiring a large, very popular, very traditional company and a smaller, more avant-garde and casual shop. The traditional florist set us up with huge photo albums of arrangements to choose from and not a live flower in sight; the "experimental" florist met with us in a corner of her greenhouse and used cut flowers piled on every available surface to illustrate our options. Dave and I chose the latter florist, because we felt, as do many soon-to-be marrieds, that flowers are just that, flowers, not floral arrangements. The last thing we wanted was some stupendous FTD sculpture readying for takeoff at the center of each table.

The only problem is, the more original florists are, the less likely they are to listen to and understand your needs. While we knew what we didn't want (who am I kidding? *I* knew; Dave couldn't have cared less), we had no vocabulary with which to describe what we did want. When I showed the florist pictures of arrangements and bouquets cut out from wedding magazines, she looked at one and said, "I've got it. You don't like weedy arrangements." I replied, "Exactly! No weeds!" Then she looked at the next picture and said, "Oh, of course. What you want is a weedy English garden style."

The best florists will be able to pick up on whatever it is you like about what you see, even if you seem to be showing contradictory pictures. For them, that means making the time to figure out what's going on in your head. While the first florist we interviewed would have done exactly what we wanted, as long as it matched one of their cookie-cutter design options, the second florist really had no patience for my lack of botanical knowledge. So what do you do when you're faced with the same situation? Exactly. You throw up your hands, write out a check, and hope for the best.

At various points, here's what I asked for in my flowers:

1. roses in plain glass bowls

2. all-white flowers;

3. no cheap fillers like carnations or daisies or daylilies

4. nothing huge

To which our florist replied:

1. Too low.

2. Too boring.

3. On your budget? Pah! But we'll try.

4. On your budget? Of course not.

The florist fought and won the glass bowl battle and we compromised on the color issue after she showed me some exotic looking things in deep purples and burgundy reds. To get rid of the daisies and carnations, I cut corners elsewhere in the budget and gave her ten dollars more to work with for each centerpiece. Still, what showed up at the wedding were mammoth bouquets of bright pink daylilies and tangerine roses. Not a purple or red in the bunch. Apparently she had sunk my extra ten dollars into more, cheaper flowers rather than fewer, expensive flowers. Were they pretty? Of course. There's no such thing as an ugly flower. Were they remotely what I wanted? Nope. Did the guests know the difference? No way.

Some people feel that, at the end of the day, flowers just aren't as important as really top quality food or a fabulous band. Flowers cost a ridiculous amount of money, and few people will, in retrospect, notice that you had $50 centerpieces instead of $150 ones. If, on the other hand, you feel the visual style of your wedding is absolutely crucial, I recommend getting a good education in flower identification before you hire your florist.

One final tip: Remember to keep your bridal bouquet to a reasonable size. You'll have to carry it all the way down the aisle—probably with your hands trembling—and then stand there with it for the duration of the ceremony. My friend Laura's bouquet was so heavy she says she could barely hold up her wrist. My own bouquet was so dense that when I tossed it behind me to all our single guests, it beaned one of them hard on the head without shaking loose a single petal. Tradition holds that our lucky guest was next in line to be married, and she was glad to hear it—as soon as she stopped feeling so dizzy.

· *His* ·

FLOWERS

Most men spend the traditional visit to the wedding florist reading the sports page, looking up only when someone coughs up a dollar amount. I say that's a big mistake. Not because the flowers at your wedding will be terrible if you don't intervene—your fiancée isn't likely to choose skunk cabbage without your guidance, after all—but because I think you'll find the experience an impressive business lesson. After the wedding, you may even want to pop a few daisies in the ground and open up shop.

Think about it. Every wedding needs floral decorations for the ceremony; bouquets, corsages, boutonnieres, petals for the flower girl, and arrangements and centerpieces for the reception. The average wedding means thousands of dollars to a florist—and no doubt there are lots of weddings in your area, not to mention high school proms, class reunions, funerals, anniversaries, and the occasional husband trying to get out of the doghouse. Somebody's making some serious cash here, so you'd better listen carefully if you want to enter the fascinating field of floristry... flowerostromy... uh, the flower sciences.

The first thing any self-respecting florist needs to do is make you, the customer, feel stupid. The flowers you think you want are obviously all wrong, wrong, wrong. You're not taking into account the season, the colors of the room, the bride's astrological sign, or the economic situation in Argentina. And you're not thinking big enough. Everybody invited to the wedding needs personal flowers, and they need really *big* personal flowers. A whole crop of 'em.

Unfortunately, at your wedding, you're not the florist; you're the sucker. And if your budget is tight, you have to play the heavy as well. You have to say no to aunts, great-aunts, and distant cousins getting corsages, no to giant chrysanthemums on the lapels of the groomsmen, no to personal flowers for new wives and husbands of remarried parents, no to a flowering arbor that covers the ceiling. Let's face it, you can spend a lot of money on flowers that not one guest will ever remember seeing. Tight budget or not, your best floral value is to cover the basics with spare, high-quality arrangements, and cover just the key players with understated corsages and boutonnieres.

If you've chosen a large room for your wedding and you can't afford to fill it with fresh flowers, find out if you can rent big green plants for the day from the building manager or the florist. Vegetation doesn't need to be flowery to create a festive atmosphere. And, the heartier the plants the better, since your guests will more than likely use the pots for ashtrays anyway.

When it comes to the bridal bouquet, it makes sense to go a little over budget. This is the one flower arrangement everyone will pay attention to, especially if your fiancée decides to do nice things with it, like plucking a flower out to give to her mother and mother-in-law on her way down the aisle. As a practical guy, you may find it strange to spend all kinds of money on something your bride is literally going to throw away. But the bridal bouquet is an important focal point of a wedding and not something you want to keep anyway (unless you have a special affection for a dried-up old ball of dead flowers).

As for determining the exact genus and species of the flowers to be used in your wedding, you might as well go back to the sports page. Your fiancée and the florist probably have much more to say about the matter than you do.

Hers

THE CAKE

WHEN you think of a wedding cake, how do you imagine it looks? Beautiful, snowy white, covered in flowers.... Now think of the taste. Ever taken a swig of straight vanilla extract because it smells so good? You get smacked with a bitter taste that sucks every drop of moisture from your throat. Gorgeous wedding cakes often offer the same delightful sensation. In fact, it seems the better a cake looks, the worse it tastes.

By the time they get married, most couples have sampled so many awful cakes at other people's weddings that when it comes time to order their own, they make taste a priority over appearance. Frosting and flowers may cover a multitude of visible sins, but nothing can disguise buttercream that tastes like lard. Recognizing this, bakers often try to sell you on a host of exotic, mouthwatering cake flavors. The best one I heard was something like "orange-hazelnut praline with white chocolate–raspberry ganache and a Belgian dark chocolate garnish." I have no idea what that would have tasted like, but I know that what Dave and I ended up with—plain white cake with plain white frosting—went over just fine with our guests.

The point is, cake isn't one of those things you need to get all worked up about. Sure, if you have the budget, you can have something made that's absolutely extraordinary. We've heard about a wedding cake completely covered with edible 14k gold foil; another one that was—no lie—at least ten feet tall; and even an Eiffel Tower made entirely of sticky buns. People love to ooh and aah at exceptionally beautiful cakes, but it's not like they'll point their finger and snicker if your cake doesn't look like the Queen Mary. One couple used a small traditional white cake solely for the cake-cutting ceremony, then, for dessert, they served their guests a choice of tiramisù, chocolate mousse, or miniature wedding cupcakes. Another couple ended up with a three-layer Duncan Hines cake made by one of the bridesmaids because the professional baker backed out at the last minute. The consequences? The couple received more compliments about the cake than any other part of their wedding.

Regardless of what your cake looks or tastes like, there is one crucial cake-oriented decision that you and your fiancé must make before your wedding. And on this you should be in *complete* agreement. Months before our reception, Dave and I carefully negotiated a no-cake-in-the-face policy. I think we actually reminded each other about it when we were standing up there getting married. Unfortunately, at the moment of cake-cutting truth, it was as though a twig snapped and we each thought it was a gunshot from the other side. There was no outright smushing or jamming, but frosting was smeared—just a tiny bit—and we never could piece together who started it or why. To this day, our wedding album includes a delightful picture of us staging a cold war near our freshly cut cake, each holding a sugary chunk at arm's length.

His

THE CAKE

DURING weddings in ancient Roman times, a small wheat cake was broken over the bride's head to ensure her fertility. Today, a large piece of frosting-smothered cake is smashed in the bride's face to ensure her humiliation. *Good piece-of-cake advice #1* is to avoid this frat-boyish prank at your own wedding. You're celebrating the beginning of a harmonious life together, so it makes no sense at all to start off with a fight.

Good piece-of-cake advice #2: Always sample a baker's or caterer's wares before you decide to let that company make your wedding cake. A baker will show you a hundred glossy photos of gorgeous cakes he's created, but the only way you'll know if they taste like shellac is to get out your fork and dig in. Besides, your reaction to looking at cake pictures is a lot like your reaction to picking out invitations, flowers, or bridesmaids' dresses: whatever is in front of you right now seems fine. But cake tasting, now that's something that requires a man's expertise. With a palate as refined as yours, it could take hours, even days, for the cakemaker to show you the perfect cake for your wedding.

Tell the prospective cakemaker he doesn't have to stick to showing you a traditional white cake either. Maybe a slice of carrot cake, German chocolate cake, cheesecake, or rum cake will suit your wedding better, or maybe a combination of many flavors, a different one for each cake tier. You'll certainly have to sample one of each. On your wedding day, there's no need to limit yourself when it comes to dessert. Maybe the cake should have an extra tier for each year you've known your fiancée, or you could have it decorated with your favorite candy (M&Ms make for a delicious, if trashy, flourish). For that matter, why stop with just one cake?

Which brings us to *good piece-of-cake advice #3*: Ask your fiancée to consider a groom's cake. This is a smaller cake of a different flavor from the wedding cake itself, and it's served at the same time. The groom's cake adds a little personality and fun to the cake-cutting ritual, because it's typically supposed to represent something the groom loves. My groom's cake, for instance, was shaped like a baseball. Having two cakes also gives your guests a choice for dessert; or, if you prefer not to turn it into a competition, you can serve the bride's cake at the reception and put slices of the groom's cake in boxes for each guest to take home.

Finally, *good piece-of-cake advice #4*: it may be a tradition to save the top tier of your wedding cake in the freezer and eat it on your first anniversary, but to many couples, the idea doesn't sound all that appetizing. I don't know anyone who actually remembered to eat that cake a year after the wedding, so why not dig into it the evening you return home from your honeymoon? I guarantee your wedding cake will taste a lot better at 14 days old than it would at 365.

·*Hers*·

ALCOHOL

SERVING alcohol at a wedding is an unexpectedly landmine-fraught topic, and as such it deserves a chapter all by itself. You'd think it would be a simple matter of whatever the groom's parents want, they get, since traditionally, they are supposed to foot the bill for alcohol at the reception. But what if your parents are teetotalers and they don't want anyone at the wedding to drink? What if your fiancé's parents don't drink, but your parents insist they pay for an open bar because it's technically their responsibility?

People are oddly dogmatic when it comes to serving alcohol. Tracy's father, for example, was adamant that no alcohol be served at her wedding, and the parents of the groom, Joe, didn't care one way or the other. But Joe wanted alcohol to be served, so he put his foot down and decided that he would foot the bill himself. At that point Tracy's father decided that if there was to going be liquor, it had to be name brands, which Joe could barely afford. What a nightmare!

Another thing that makes serving alcohol tough is that wherever there's vodka, there's a jerk who drinks way too much—and that jerk could be your husband. There's a wedding legend about one bride whose husband got smashed at the reception, then fell into the lobby fountain on the way to their hotel room. After opening the complimentary bottle of champagne in their suite, he passed out cold. Of course, brides and grooms alike are susceptible to alcohol-induced amnesia, which is the last thing you want on your wedding day. Imagine how awful it would be to remember absolutely nothing about your reception because you drank two glasses of wine after having been too nervous to eat for the preceding three days.

Most people expect alcohol at a wedding, so by all means have it, as long as it adds to the festivity and assuming you, or whoever is paying, can afford it. But keep in mind that there's no mandate to serve drinks. If you or either set of parents has a strong moral or religious objection to alcohol, or if your wedding is simply too early in the morning for an open bar, it's both economical and appropriate to offer an open juice, soda, and punch bar complete with virgin mimosas and piña coladas. A nonalcoholic sparkling wine is an acceptable substitute for champagne.

The most important thing is that you feel comfortable at your reception. You may worry that people won't have fun unless they're able to drink, but at the same time you don't want to be nervous about dealing with falling-down drunks. If you decide to limit the amount of alcohol at your reception, be confident that your guests will take care of themselves. The ones who have to drink in order to have fun will leave early, and the rest will stay on and enjoy themselves.

· *His* ·

ALCOHOL

IT'S almost a guarantee that you'll end up in charge of the liquor at your wedding. Why? Mainly because your fiancée wants to give you something to do so you'll stop bothering her. Also, dealing with alcohol is manly; there are kegs to lug, cases to unload, and shots to pour. So once it's agreed that you'll be handling all the alcohol-related decisions, you'll need to review your options. Based on availability of money, time of day, and knowledge of your guests, you may take your pick from the following:

1. *Open bar, top shelf.* This will cost big bucks, so whoever is paying for it (typically the parents of the groom or the groom himself) better have deep pockets. Free-flowing alcohol ensures a lively party from beginning to end, but be sure to appoint a member of the wedding party to be the official sober person, bathroom nurse, car key holder, and designated driver.

2. *Open bar, house brands.* For when you want your guests to drink and be merry, but you don't have the resources to spring for the very best. If money is an issue, you may want to consider closing the bar during the meal,

when guests will presumably have wine and champagne at the table anyway. Then reopen the liquor cabinet for the final hours of the reception. You can also look into a pay-for-what-your-guests-drink option, in which you're charged for only the bottles that get opened rather than a flat per-guest fee. In either case, expect to hear from your guests about harsher hangovers when you serve brands like Uncle Al's Homemade Hooch.

3. *Alcohol à la carte.* Many caterers and reception hall bartenders will serve the beer, wine, and liquor that you provide for them. You can save some serious cash this way, but of course, you have to do all the work—figuring out how much your guests will drink, finding a liquor store with good prices, making sure they have what you need in stock, arranging delivery, and chasing after them when the delivery is late. It's like clipping coupons; if you have to, you have to, but nobody really *wants* to.

4. *Beer, wine, and champagne only.* A reasonable money-saving option that should make most guests happy, but not *too* happy, if you know what I mean. Instead of tequila shots, your highly sophisticated groomsmen will have to make do with shotgunning cans of Budweiser.

5. *Cash bar.* Oh boy, now you're really gonna tick some people off. Not only do most guests find paying for drinks at your wedding incredibly tacky, it's the kind of thing that makes them think they spent too much on your gift. If money is a problem, it's far better to go with free drinks for a limited time, or no alcohol at all, than it is to make your guests pull out their own wallets at your party.

6. *No bar.* You often find this at morning or early afternoon receptions, or in church halls that don't allow alcohol. In these cases it makes perfect sense. It's hard for any guest to justify needing a gin and tonic at eleven A.M. on a Sunday, and since most aren't expecting an early wedding to be an all-day affair, they would just as soon go home and have their own beer without all the formalwear. Expect early exits and not a lot of dancing.

7. *Extras.* Sometimes the champagne toast and dinner wines are included in the price of the food, sometimes not. Make sure you check, because these are the kind of major unforeseen expenses that can mess things up at the last minute. In general, a pricey dinner wine is a waste of

Seven Survival Tips for Making the Toast

Clip this out and hand it to your best man—preferably before he writes his own toast.

1. No ex-girlfriend stories. Nobody will think they're funny except you.
2. Keep it to 200 words or less. This isn't your own HBO special.
3. Express your deep affection for the bride, even if you hate her guts.
4. Nervous hands will shake, so don't pick up the champagne until you're almost done.
5. If you want to live through the meal, remember the bride's name.
6. Play to both sexes. Try for laughs from the men, and tears from the women.
7. The jokes should come out of your mouth; make sure your fly is zipped.

money. As long as it doesn't come out of a box, most of your guests won't notice that their Chardonnay doesn't have a pedigree.

Once you handle the decision on the scope of alcohol to be served at your wedding, there's one final choice to make. How much of it will you drink? While you may feel compelled to sample every available type of liquor you've sanctioned in order to, you know, see if it's up to snuff, no one makes a bigger target for reproach than a drunk groom, especially to a blushing bride with a handful of wedding cake. You wouldn't want her to be overblushed from five too many glasses of zinfandel, would you?

Too much alcohol at your wedding reception is a recipe for disaster: you're both nervous; neither of you have eaten all day and possibly all week; you're in a social situation where you have to visit, dance, play host, and have a great time; and all these factors can combine to speed alcohol to your brain faster than you can say Jägermeister. Before you know it, you have your head in the toilet, and that's nobody's idea of a romantic finale to the happiest day of your life. So go easy on the alcohol at your own party, then pop the cork once you arrive at your honeymoon destination.

·*Hers*·

FRILLS, FURBELOWS, AND FAVORS

IF I had to name the aspect of a traditional wedding that makes the least sense, it would be those little things you're supposed to put by every place setting at the reception. Miniature picture frames, teensy unidentifiable crystal objects... for some reason, it's perfectly acceptable to give away as wedding favors items that are patently unusable and practically scream, "Throw me away when you get home!" You name it, and some couple has probably bought it in bulk engraved with hearts and flowers.

Then again, the couple probably wasn't the culprit, but rather the mother of the bride. MOBs are inexplicably big on favors; at some point in the wedding planning process they seem to lose sight of the fact that the reception is meant to be a *reception*. MOBs quickly drift back to their Junior Prom Planning Committee days, to all those happy hours spent hanging crepe paper stars and balloons. It's an easy mistake: After all, the two of you have probably been discussing the colors of the bridesmaids' dresses and flowers, and from there, it's just one tiny nostalgic step to color-coordinating balloons, napkins, and punch. Since every MOB still has her treasured champagne flute engraved with the date of her prom squirreled away in the attic, you know she's going to want only the best in party favors for her guests.

"But Mom," you cry, "they're not your guests, they're my guests! And this isn't the prom, it's a party celebrating my wedding!"

"My point exactly," your mother replies calmly. "All parties have favors. Remember the miniature teacups we gave away on your birthday? Those were such a hit."

"I was ten," you say. "Things have changed!"

I have yet to meet a bride who's won the party favor argument. Just try telling your mother that favors are useless, that guests may not want to display knickknacks or use coffee mugs with your name on them, that in fact giving favors puts guests in the uncomfortable position of not wanting to throw away the treasured memento of your special day but having absolutely no purpose for a solitary monogrammed place card holder. If your mother is a favor kind of gal, then favors you will have. The best you can hope for is having some input as to what they will be and how much they will cost, since moms tend to get so swept up in the adorableness of the favor that they forget they have to multiply its unit cost by number of guests.

"Look, honey! It's a teensy sterling silver jelly pot with a little circle for you to put your wedding picture in. It's perfect!"

"It's twenty dollars. We have 150 guests."

"Well, how about we just do away with the open bar and get those hand-kerchiefs for everyone silkscreened with your engagement picture? They were only ten dollars."

An informal survey of wedding guests will tell you that the most appreci-ated giveaways are either genuinely useful or consumable items. Small boxes of Godiva chocolate may not be terribly original, but you know they'll be eaten. One couple we know gave away small packages of Fig Newtons because, as all their friends knew, the groom proposed in front of the New-tons in their grocery store's cookie aisle. Votive candles will probably be burned, regardless of whether they have your name on them and, unless they're hideous, Christmas ornaments will likely be hung on the tree. Some couples give away little packets of flower seeds, which are both symbolic and functional.

If you really think about it, there are ways to make wedding favors useful and interesting. On this issue—as with all aspects of wedding planning—if you can't beat your mother, join her. Just make sure it's on terms you can live with.

· *His* ·

FRILLS, FURBELOWS, AND FAVORS

THE folks who came up with the idea of party favors must have had a lot of extra time and money on their hands. The thinking probably went something like this: people go to weddings, they bring gifts, they should leave with gifts too. Apparently it's not enough for you to provide everyone you know with free food, drink, entertainment, and floral centerpieces. You have to send them home with a personalized candle snifter too. Better still, you have to spend hours deciding whether a snifter is more appropriate for your wedding than the chocolate-covered blueberries wrapped in ribbon. Or maybe you should put something more personal at each guest's place setting, like a framed copy of a poem the bride wrote in third grade.

Most couples end up offering lousy party gifts because trinkets are cheap when you buy them in bulk, and nobody wants to spend a fortune on something that's basically an afterthought. Regrettably, if you insist on offering wedding favors (or the mother of the bride insists for you) there are only two guaranteed ways to make them good: spend a fortune, or make sure they're not an afterthought.

No doubt your wedding planner or caterer will have a whole catalog of suggestions for elegant wedding favors your guests can actually use, such as sterling silver picture frames or crystal vases. Providing a nice gift like this for each guest will only cost you your firstborn. Engraving the date of your wedding on these items not only increases the cost, it will leave your guests scratching their heads five years from now when they try to figure out the significance of that date on the picture frame that holds the smiling visage of dear departed Uncle Pippy.

The other party favor route—keeping it from being an afterthought—holds much more promise for the creative husband-and-wife-to-be. With some concentrated brainstorming early on, you can come up with a gift that's just the right combination of inexpensive, interesting, personal, fun, useful, and available in quantities of a hundred or more. How about a CD single of your first dance song? Or a miniature book of poetry by someone frequently quoted at weddings, such as e. e. cummings or Kahlil Gibran? Snacks are always a good idea, preferably something unique or homemade that reflects your ethnic background. We've seen cubes of Turkish delight at a Turkish wedding, candy-coated almonds at a Greek wedding, halvah at a Jewish wedding, and miniatures of scotch at a Scottish wedding—all perfectly appropriate and delicious.

If you can't think of any favors that you like or that you can afford to offer, my advice is to skip them altogether, and don't let anyone guilt you into something frilly and silly at the last minute. In the entire history of weddings, not one guest has ever gone home moaning that he didn't get a party favor, but plenty have left stupid knickknacks lying right there on the table. If you can't think of something that's absolutely perfect for the occasion, spend that extra money on a wider variety of hors d'oeuvres. That'll be doing yourselves and your guests a real favor.

· *Hers* ·

PHOTOGRAPHERS AND VIDEOGRAPHERS

AFTER your wedding, you may look around and wonder what you have to show for it. Aside from some stray pieces of birdseed stuck in your hair, a stack of outrageous bills, a pile of gifts, and a lump of wilted flowers that used to be your bouquet (unless you threw it), there isn't much tangible evidence of the five hours that capped off a year's worth of obsessive planning. Sure, you have a partner for life. But the human memory is short and fleeting, and ten years down the road, when you're fighting over mortgages and hedge trimmers and diapers, it would be nice to recall, with perfect clarity, that long-ago moment of declaring your love for each other in front of a packed house.

Enter the professional photographer and videographer. You might think all photographers are the same; after all, it's not as though you have to choose between hiring Rembrant and Picasso to immortalize your big day. Photography is realism, not art. All these people have to do is point and shoot, right? Wrong. Wedding photographers have very individual senses of taste and style, and their artistic vision will completely color the record of your wedding for eternity. This is why it's important to evaluate the work of a variety of photographers, and choose the one whose pictures are most evocative of your personal style. As many brides learn from experience, it's a bad idea to pick one and expect him to adapt to you.

Here are the basic categories into which most photographers fit:

Old Faithful. This guy has worked every notable wedding in town. Your caterer, minister, and florist know him by name. He's practically on-staff at the local reception hall. He offers you a pricing structure that reads like the back of a Chinese menu: package A, package B, or package C. Hiring this guy will require absolutely no effort on your part—he knows what he's doing, and he assures you that you'll end up with every possible picture you could ever want. On the other hand, if you ask him to do something unusual, such as taking a couple of black-and-white photographs during the wedding, he'll look at you like you have two heads. His favorite shot is the one where he has you pose with your bridesmaids admiring your newly wedding-beringed finger, or seated under a tree in the churchyard with your skirt artfully fanned out around you.

The Upstart. She was tops in her community college course on How to Start Your Own Business as a Wedding Photographer, and now that her kids are off to school, she's been enjoying some modest success working out of her home. You show up in her living room and she hauls out a box of what look to you to be family snapshots, but which she proudly tells you are samples of some of her finest jobs. She's recently mastered high-tech tricks of the trade such as blurring the edges of shots to frame the bride and groom in a fuzzy oval halo, or adding props, like a Victorian parasol or a puppy. If you hire her, you'll have write down every single photograph you want. On the plus side, she's cheap, cheap, cheap. But don't forget to bring extra film and a camera to your wedding. That's one of those little details she might overlook in the excitement of the day.

The Artiste. Don't ever make the mistake of calling this guy a wedding photographer. He is willing, however, to attend your wedding and take photographs as the spirit moves him. Do not expect him to take a picture of you with your mother or your husband with his groomsmen. He may not even take a picture of you with your husband. But he will record the light shining from your wedding band onto your raised fork, and you may get a stunning shot of your tulle veil floating onto an aesthetically pleasing lineup of all the ushers' shiny shoes.

The No-show. He seems like a nice enough guy, but after you give him your deposit, he skips town. Of course, he's nice enough not to let you know that he's gone until you try to reach him a day before the wedding. One variant on this incarnation of evil is the guy who actually shows up at your wedding and takes pictures, then disappears from the face of the earth. Six months after their wedding, one couple we spoke with still hasn't seen their proofs.

For our wedding, Dave and I interviewed what felt like a hundred photographers, and found that the good ones were too expensive and the affordable ones were awful. We groaned collectively when my mother suggested we talk to some friends of hers, a husband and wife team—from her amateur photography club. But we were blown away by their work and loved the fact that they were commercial and nature photographers, not experienced wedding photographers. We made a small list of the shots we wanted and then let them go to town. In the end, they took stunning pictures using traditional color film, black and white film, and even infrared. So when it comes to photography, explore all your options. Quality is what counts, not tradition.

As for wedding videos, if you have one professionally made, it's going to be a little cheesy, no matter who shoots it. You can spend a lot of time and money researching videographers, but at the end of the day what you really want is something that records what your wedding was like, in live action, since you'll probably be too freaked out at the time to notice what's going on. If you go with a professional, ask the videographer not to get carried away with so many artistic cuts and fades that you lose the main action. Another option is to ask someone on the guest list whether he would consider it a pleasure or a duty to bring along a minicam. Just make sure he's trustworthy. Who knows what you'll get if you assume Uncle Leo can handle the videocamera between chugging champagne and ogling the ladies.

· *His* ·

PHOTOGRAPHERS AND
VIDEOGRAPHERS

"Hi. I'm the wedding photographer you found in the Yellow Pages. I'm a fifty-eight-year-old male with a bad toupee and big tinted glasses. As you can see by the sofa-sized blow ups on my studio wall, I've been doing this for quite some time, and I have a special affinity for the styles of the seventies. I've got a take-charge attitude and I plan to get close enough to see your pores at the moment you say 'I do.'

"I'm a kidder. I like to kid, so I'm likely to loosen things up a bit by saying 'Okay, people, look at the birdie and say Parcheesi!' or 'Alrighty, only two thousand more shots to go!' Yep, I'm a real hoot. Did I mention I charge three thousand dollars for a wedding of your size? And for that price, I'll throw so much romantic haze onto the prints, you'll barely recognize yourselves."

WHY do so many couples settle for wedding photographers like this when, with a little careful research, they can usually find someone cheaper who'll take more interesting pictures and be a lot less obtrusive? Probably because most people are scared to death to trust their one-of-a-kind photographs to someone who hasn't been shooting weddings since the Ice Age. So these couples are forced to follow a checklist of "required shots" that the photographer slogs through—1) bride coming down aisle, 2) mother of bride crying, 3) priest saying, 'til death do you part, 4) groom crying—and they end up with a photo album filled with generic memories that serve only to remind them that, yes, a few years ago, a wedding did occur.

So what are the alternatives to the Photosaurus Rex? Some couples go with a friend or relative who has a picture-taking bent. While this is certainly a cheap option, you may not get the best results, and that person will be so busy working that he won't have time to enjoy the wedding. Local camera clubs are filled with a wide range of aspiring photographers, many with their own professional equipment and development labs, who would be happy to work your wedding for a reasonable fee. Often these amateur shutterbugs are more willing to listen to your own personal list of must-have pictures, and more likely to capture creative shots you never would have dreamed up.

If you decide to go with a professional wedding photographer, you don't have to go with the biggest name in town or the first one you see. Ask for recommendations from a caterer or wedding planner whom you like. Shop around, and when you visit the photographer's studio, look beyond the sample wedding albums. Does it look like the place has been redecorated sometime in the last decade? Do the photographs on the wall look like they came out of a wallet? Does this photographer specialize in volume or does he limit himself to only a few weddings each month? Will the person you're talking to be the actual photographer at your wedding?

Once you've found the right person or team for the job, you have to decide when the pictures should be taken. Photographs are the one part of a wedding that isn't for immediate consumption. No one enjoys taking time out of this important day to pose for the cameras. In fact, while the photographer is capturing on film every possible combination of family members, friends, pets, and floral arrangements, the rest of the guests are wasting away from hunger, wondering if dinner is ever going to be served.

To lighten the postceremony burden on photographer and guests alike, keep the bar open for your guests during the photographic lull. For the wedding party being photographed, ask a waiter or some distant cousin to keep the gin and tonics coming. Alternatively, many couples choose to take the majority of their pictures before the ceremony gets started—or at least those that don't involve both bride and groom at the same time. You don't want to see your bride in her dress before she marches down the aisle because that's twelve thousand years of bad luck... or something. Mostly, it's just bad luck for the photographer who can never move fast enough to make everyone happy.

Disposable cameras on each table at the reception can be both a blessing and a curse. On the one hand, your guests will take pictures your photographer couldn't possibly get, and if your professional photographs are a disappointment, those your guests provide could be a saving grace. On the other hand, your guests may take pictures you couldn't possibly want, like a close-up of someone's nostril, an arty shot of the camera-holder's left shoe, or the best man mooning you for good luck.

Finally, we come to the wedding video, something you could easily spend a small fortune on and only watch once, probably under duress. If your or your bride's parents insist on a video, it's only fair that they pay for and arrange it. No matter who pays, however, you'll end up giving direction to the videographer yourself, and that can be a painful process. One couple told their male cameraman to get all the guests on film—which he dutifully did, paying extremely close attention to the breasts and posteriors of the females. When told to get a shot of every table, he performed exactly as asked. Watching their video two weeks after the wedding, the bride and groom were treated to a slow, careful pan across every single table. No guests, mind you, just twenty-four tables perfectly preserved on film.

PHOTOGRAPHERS AND VIDEOGRAPHERS

· *Hers* ·

THE OFFICIANT

BLESSED is the couple who knows their wedding officiant well. Whether it's the minister whose church the bride has attended since she was a child or the groom's uncle Jim (a pastor who happens to work in tandem with the cantor from the bride's synagogue), the nuptial ceremony is always extra special when its officiant speaks from the heart about the loving couple.

Such ceremonies have that personal touch, revealing a bit of inside information about the bride or groom that's guaranteed to make either the guests or the newlyweds squirm in embarrassment. For example, Elena and Ted, who had together attended the requisite Catholic marriage preparatory classes, got this surprise at their wedding ceremony: before all two hundred guests, the priest who had overseen the classes said, "I can't tell you how delighted I am to see Ted and Elena arriving at this moment. You see, for the longest time, Elena has been sure of her decision and ready to be married, but Ted has been having many second thoughts. Praise God for helping him overcome his great doubts and grow up enough to be ready for this lifelong commitment."

It could have been worse. We attended one wedding in which the rabbi said, "We all thought Rachel was a lesbian when she was a child, and this happy day marks the moment when we can put that rumor to rest." That one was neck and neck with the minister who remarked, "No one in Mary's family ever thought she would find someone who would put up with her for the rest of her life. So from the bottom of her heart, her mother wants to thank Steven for saving her from the convent—although I know the Little Sisters of Charity would have been happy to have Mary in the flock."

If you don't have a family pastor or minister or rabbi, you can either befriend the officiant of the church in which you will be having your ceremony or seek recommendations from friends who speak highly of their family's clergyman or -woman. For couples who either cannot agree upon a particular religious faith in which to conduct their ceremony or who don't have a strong religious background, it's easy to hire a secular officiant such as a justice of the peace or a judge. There are also organizations such as the Ethical Culture Society, through which you can hire an officiant who will perform a ceremony with whatever philosophical undercurrents you agree upon. In these cases, an officiant is no further away than the phone book.

Whether you are married in an ultratraditional religious ceremony or by a judge according to vows you have written yourself, it's always a good idea to explain to your guests the meaning behind your choice of officiant and ceremony, perhaps as a note in your wedding program. Of course, if you're married by the Minister of Black Death at a Satanist convention or by the captain of the S.S. *Sea Chanty* where you're spending your vacation, no explanation is necessary.

SEVEN SURVIVAL TIPS FOR WHEN YOUR OFFICIANT EMBARRASSES YOU

1. Remind him that God is watching.
2. He may remember you in diapers, but, unlike him, at least you're not wearing them now.
3. Tell him the best man's packing heat.
4. Bop him on the head with your bouquet.
5. Inform him that you can see right up his robe.
6. Oh, no! The caterers seem to have misplaced his dinner.
7. One more embarrassing comment, and there goes your tip.

· *His* ·

THE OFFICIANT

THERE are only four things you absolutely, positively *need* in order to get married: a bride, a license, a witness, and an officiant—someone to legally pronounce you husband and wife. These authority figures run the gamut from archbishops to Elvis impersonators, and they come in both genders, varying personalities, and every denominational flavor, including nondenominational. Your officiant may be a trusted religious leader from childhood, a respected official from your fiancée's community, or a justice of the peace whom neither of you have ever met. No matter where they come from, officiants set the tone for the weddings they perform, and so at least part of your decision about the person who marries you should be based on his performance ability.

If your preferred officiant speaks often at your church, temple, or mosque, it's easy to research his skill at conveying emotional material and captivating a crowd. If the person you want to have marry you and your fiancée performs nightly in the Las Vegas Blue Suede Shoe Revue, you know you're in for one rockin' wedding. Many couples get a pretty good idea of what their officiant will be like during the ceremony just by meeting him once or twice before the wedding. Beyond that, you'll have to trust that he knows more about weddings than you do, and that he will do everything possible to make your ceremony special.

If you're feeling obsessive and you want to leave nothing up to chance, request a copy of the ceremony and vows your officiant usually reads, and do some thoughtful editing to make sure nothing is included that you find disagreeable or offensive. Your officiant will probably need some space to say something personal about the two of you, and if he doesn't know you very well, you may want to provide autobiographical tidbits to help out. Most officiants are quite good at making it seem like you're the favorite disciples in their personal flock. Performing weddings has to be one of the most enjoyable parts of anyone's job description, so after a certain point you should loosen your grip on the ceremony and let the officiant run with it.

Despite all your efforts to procure a reasonably normal officiant, on your wedding day, you may find that your fearless leader falls into one of these scary categories:

The Comedian. This hip and happenin' religious leader likes to reach out to all the young dudes and dudettes out there by interspersing all that hard-to-swallow faith stuff with a few well-placed funnies. Sometimes it works, and sometimes it's like Pat Boone singing AC/DC.

The True Believer. Silly you. You thought it was the bride and groom's special day. Well, you couldn't be more wrong. Today, and every day, is *God's* special day, and this officiant just received a telegram from the all-powerful one himself expressing His joy that the betrothed will be living under His watchful eye until Judgment Day. Just try consummating your marriage after a few hours of this.

The Teacher. Want to know why nuptial couples exchange rings? Ever wonder why the bride wears a veil? Interested in what makes this officiant's yellow ducky boxer shorts particularly lucky? He will be happy to explain it all to you right in the middle of the ceremony. A few goys in the audience? Here's a brief history of Judaism. Don't speak Latin? No problem. He'll go over the whole one-hour ceremony again in English.

The Geriatric. Why did his mouth stop moving? Is he dead? No. Whew! Just took a quick nap. There he goes again, at a one-word-a-minute pace about how he proudly married the bride's mother, her mother, and her mother before her. He vowed he would live long enough to officiate his fourth generation of Weinentraub weddings, and thanks to the wonders of cryogenic science, he just might make it through the reception.

Little Miss Crystal. Now appearing, fresh from an engagement in Sedona, Arizona, is the reincarnation of Lady Godiva. Thanking everyone present for contributing to the karmic balance of the room, she's guaranteed to align the bride and groom's chakras with the spiritual assistance of Vishnu and Verna, her life partner of many years. Numerologically speaking, the couple couldn't have picked a more perfect day, and thank the stars, the Virgo/Taurus union is notoriously harmonious.

Even if your officiant turns out to be one of these wackos, you're guaranteed an interesting ceremony. At least you'll have something to laugh about with your buddies (once your new wife stops crying).

THE BUILD-A-FAKE-WEDDING GAME

The purpose of playing this game is to practice putting together your own wedding without spending any real money. In real life, you might have a firm wedding budget limit of fifteen thousand dollars; in this game, you have a limit of fifty points. The two of you play the parts of (surprise!) bride and groom. Together, you must discuss each key wedding element in the list below and "buy" one thing from each category for the indicated number of points. At the end of the game, you want to come as close to fifty as you can without going over. Just as in real life, you may have to sacrifice the best flowers in order to get the perfect reception hall. It's great practice for the negotiations you're about to encounter.

Total Budget: 50 points

The Key Elements	Points
Room Rental	
a) Mom and Dad's backyard	0
b) Joe's Diner/Polka House	2
c) A local reception hall	5
d) A historic mansion	10
Food/Catering	
a) Potluck dinner	0
b) Pasta and salad buffet	5
c) Sit-down chicken and fish	10
d) Five courses/prime rib/wait staff	20

Invitations
a) Make 'em yourself on the computer — 1
b) Back of the invitation book — 2
c) Front of the invitation book — 4
d) Custom-made by a local artist — 8

Music
a) Your friend, the DJ — 2
b) Your friend's wedding band — 4
c) A professional wedding band — 8
d) A really, really amazing band — 16

Flowers
a) None or handpicked — 0
b) Minimal arrangements — 5
c) Enough to fill the place — 10
d) Enough to fill the Astrodome — 20

The Cake
a) Duncan Hines — 1
b) White cake decorated with flowers — 2
c) Larger cake/marzipan everywhere — 3
d) Cake as big as the groom — 8

Alcohol
a) None — 0
b) Champagne toast/mimosa punch — 2
c) Open bar/beer and wine — 6
d) Open bar/top-shelf liquor — 9

Favors

a)	Lottery tickets	1
b)	Tiny boxes of chocolates	2
c)	Mini picture frames	5
d)	Anything from Tiffany's	8

Wedding Dress

a)	Basic gown off the rack	3
b)	Designer gown off the rack	7
c)	Specially designed just for bride	12
d)	Buy four dresses, only wear one	20

Photography/Videography

a)	Uncle Sid and Aunt Bea	1
b)	Friends from the local camera club	3
c)	Two professionals	6
d)	Annie Leibowitz	30

Officiant

a)	Minister at your church	1
b)	A justice of the peace	2
c)	A ship captain	3
d)	Captain Kirk	10

The Wedding Party

· *Hers* ·

PARENTS OF THE BRIDE

YOU'VE heard the horror stories. There's the mother who, commando-style, took over the bridal operation from start to finish, picking the date, time, and place of the ceremony, designing the bridesmaids' dresses, typing up vow treatments for the priest to choose from, and in the end getting stuck with a thirty-thousand-dollar cocktail party for her friends when the bride and groom eloped to Mexico.

On the other hand, there's also the well-intentioned but meddling parents of the perfect bride and groom, as depicted in the movie *Father of the Bride*. The bride's mother delegates everything to a foppish, fussy wedding planner-slash-artiste, and the bride's father, played by Steve Martin, runs around trying desperately to make everything perfect for his little girl. Both mother and father want nothing more than to spend bazillions of dollars on the wedding of their baby's dreams.

If your parents, like most, are contributing money toward the cost of the wedding, they may feel they've purchased the right to arrange things to suit their needs. But chances are, you don't have a father like the Steve Martin character who's happy to spend ten thousand on an ice sculpture of a swan because he thinks his daughter wants it. Sure, your father loves to see you happy. But only if your joy comes in under budget. His idea of wedding expenses were fixed in the fifties, when floral arrangements consisted of a bunch of carnations on every table, dyed to match the lime-green Jell-o appetizer and the fizzy punch. And you probably don't have a mother who will take over your wedding or delegate it to some stranger, either. In comparison to the ultimate wedding nightmares and dreams come true, the foibles and interferences of your own parents are likely to be a little more reasonable.

One father of the bride, for instance, decided that if he was paying for musical entertainment, he was going to hire the band without consulting his daughter. His terrific idea: a one-man act, consisting of accordion, harmonica, knee symbols, and bass drum, known as a gitorganist. One mother of the bride believed her monetary contribution entitled her to have final approval over her daughter's dress selection. These are annoyances, but they are not insurmountable problems.

More difficult than satisfying your parents' demands and instructions, however, is getting them to somehow follow yours. Despite repeated written directions, my father forgot to sit down after walking me down the aisle, and so, for twenty minutes on the videotape, it looks like I'm marrying Dave *and* Dad. At my friend's wedding, her mother forgot she was supposed to stick around to take formal pictures after the ceremony, and pitched a fit when she realized the photographer hadn't taken any pictures of her. So she stopped the reception and demanded a reshoot with all the key members of the wedding.

Sadly, there are no words of wisdom to help you cope with your parents during the planning of your wedding. If they're paying for it, they're probably going to drive you nuts. When you accept their money, you tacitly accept their interference. Fortunately, you can always turn to your fiancé for moral support.

What things cost	What your father thought was reasonable
Dinner: $80 a plate	$200 total. A couple of those 6-foot-long subs, and we're all set.
Bar tab: $2,000	Free. They can bring their own beer, like I do to the ball-game.
Flowers: $3,000	Your mother has a beautiful garden, and a pretty good knack for arranging posies.
The band: $2,500	$100. Honey, did I mention I saw this guitorganist...
Cake: $800	$4.95. Hell, I can bake a cake myself.
Wedding dress: $2,000	Well, let's see. Your mother's cost $250. Hey! Why don't you wear hers? It was from Sears—guaranteed to last.

· *His* ·
....
PARENTS OF THE BRIDE

No two people hold more power and influence over your wedding than do the father and mother of the bride. If you're not close to them now, believe me, you will be by the time you say "I do."

Allow me to do the introductions. First, meet your future father-in-law. Since the day his daughter was born, he's hated the very thought of you. He's always feared that some day some young punk would meet his little girl, and then court her, sleep with her, and marry her leaving him with the honor of paying for it all. He will allow you to do all of that to his daughter on two conditions: you have a good job, and you treat her like an angel.

Given this man's financial and emotional stake in your marriage, it's best to handle him with the utmost respect. Invite him to a football game or out for a round of golf. Chat him up at family gatherings. Ask him for permission to marry his daughter. And make sure he's included in the bachelor party.

Traditionally, the bride's parents will pay for all wedding expenses except the rings, the honeymoon, the rehearsal dinner, the bride's bouquet, and alcohol at the reception, but that's not set in stone. Many couples ask the groom's parents to contribute half of the total costs or more, and quite a few couples finance their own wedding. Even so, it's more than likely that your new dad-in-law will take the hardest financial hit, so here are two things you can do to keep him happy: One, offer him a major role in the ceremony, such as walking his daughter down the aisle and giving her away. For many men, this is the proudest moment of their lives. Two, let your fiancée's father pick the song for the father-daughter dance. Or at least discuss it with him. For a father of the bride, this is the most emotional part of the wedding, and the last thing he wants is a song he's never heard and can't dance to.

Now meet your future mother-in-law; the other woman you'll be marrying. From the moment you announce your engagement, she springs into action, making phone calls, arranging meetings with caterers, and offering helpful "suggestions." Since her mother wouldn't let her make any decisions at her own wedding, she's going to try to run yours. Let the power struggles begin.

Most likely, this battle for domination will be harder on your fiancée than it is on you. After all, the very things her mother cares deeply about are those on which you have no opinion whatsoever. Your mother-in-law can take a great deal of pressure off you by being an endlessly enthusiastic partner with your future wife in conversations about things like table favors, boutonnieres, and the style of calligraphy on the invitations. Usually, however, the pressure is just delayed. It comes your way in a different form: Your fiancée complains to you that her mother is too pushy, or just plain stubborn. Now you've got to play referee, and no place is more dangerous to stand than between a bride and her mother when a wedding is on the line. If you're forced to intervene, take your wife's side of the argument. This is, by far, the lesser of two evils. A mother-in-law's wrath is fleeting, but an angry wife is forever.

Naturally, you should still try to keep your future mother-in-law happy whenever you can, so here are two suggestions: One, give her an important part to play in the wedding as well. Many mothers want to stand and give their daughters away, too. If not, make sure your mother-in-law is escorted down the aisle by the handsomest groomsman, preferably the best man. Two, ask her to dance during the reception. The groom always looks like the grandest of gentlemen at his own wedding, but when you extend your arm to your new mother, you'll look like a knight in shining armor.

· Hers ·

PARENTS OF THE GROOM

In addition to keeping your own mother in line and reaching for the smelling salts every time you present your parents with a bill, in planning a wedding you have to accommodate the needs of your soon-to-be second family. By and large, your future father-in-law just doesn't want to be bothered. His biggest concern is making sure everyone has a full glass and a smile on his or her face. Your fiancé's mother, however, really wishes she were the mother of the bride, not of the groom. Sure, it's hard for her to relinquish her little boy to the arms of another woman, but truth be told, what's toughest for her about watching her son get married is the fact that she's not in charge of planning it.

Never fear. There are easy ways to lull the most determined of in-laws into a contented state of noninterference without putting them under hypnosis or spiking their drinks with Valium. The key is to understand their motivations.

You may find your mother-in-law's behavior interfering and annoying, but all she really wants is to be involved. You can accommodate her by asking her out shopping for your or your bridesmaids' dresses. Who cares if you don't really want her input on the dress selection? It's a good chance for the two of you to get better acquainted, and to make her feel like she has a voice in the major wedding decisions. A mother-in-law ignored is likely to retaliate by passive resistance. Cecilia chose a wedding color scheme without consulting her mother-in-law, who nodded and smiled when asked to buy a dress that would match. Cecilia was hoping for taupe; her mother-in-law showed up in red.

It's often the case that your family and your fiancé's family come from different backgrounds, and your respective mothers are likely to have very different priorities and senses of style. So, if you want your fiancé's mother to wear a certain color dress to the wedding, you should definitely tell her. Otherwise, there's no way of knowing what she'll show up in. But a better way to accomplish the same goal is to include your mother-in-law at key points in the planning process. She may become so accommodating that she'll actually ask you what you want her to wear.

Start by asking your future mother-in-law's advice about where her family's friends and relatives should be seated during the reception. Then give her a complete project of her own to do (note: proceed with caution, since this is verging on your mother's turf). Need little birdseed sachets to hand to the guests before you make your grand exit? I can think of someone who'd love to take the task of making them off your hands. The flower girl wants a dress that's so cute you could just puke, and if your mother-in-law is a half-decent seamstress, she'd be more than happy to crank up the sewing machine. Looking for a sweet little pillow for the ringbearer? You can be sure that your mom-in-law knows how to make one. Keep in mind that if you're going to give her these assignments, you have to be prepared to relinquish control over them. Those sachets, that dress, and that pillow are going to look exactly like your fiancé's mother wants them to look. It's a small price to pay to keep control of the rest of the wedding firmly in your own hands.

And what's Dad doing this whole time? Unlike their wives, most future fathers-in-law don't want to be involved in the wedding planning. They just want to be of use. Feeling helpless in the wedding beehive of hoopla and shenanigans and melodrama, dads want to be the steady worker drones going about their own business and safely out of the way in case the queen has another tantrum. Give him a job that gets him out of the house; if you ask him where he'd like to have the rehearsal dinner, he can spend months happily having a drink in the bar of every restaurant within a two-hour radius. At the wedding itself, assign him an easy but essential responsibility—like bringing home all the wedding gifts—that will take his mind off how much he hates wearing a tuxedo.

His·

PARENTS OF THE GROOM

WHY are these two people smiling? Because a) their son will soon have someone else to make him clean up after himself, b) they finally get to see him wearing something other than that ratty T-shirt, and c) they get to attend a wedding for one of their children without having to pay for it. Yep, the parents of the groom have it pretty good. But probe a little bit deeper and you'll find that life's not all a bowl of cherries for these two.

For instance, they will pay the bill for the rehearsal dinner, for which Burger King isn't really an option. They also will feel pressure to give you a very nice gift, usually cash—sometimes earmarked for the honeymoon and sometimes for the purchase of your first home, so we're not just talking about a hundred bucks.

There's an emotional cost for your parents as well, especially for your mother. It can be tough for most mothers to lose their sons to another woman. Even if you're six-foot-eight and thirty years old, your mom probably still loves babying you, cooking you a nice meal, knitting you warm sweaters, and getting on your case about the length of your hair or the controlled chaos of your apartment. It will take her some time to adjust to the new dominant female force in your life. She may not always approve at first, and there may be more than a few tears throughout the wedding process, especially during the mother-son dance, but eventually your mother will accept your new wife as one of the family.

In the meantime, Mom will try to insinuate herself into the planning process any way she can. From her proposal to create place settings out of your baby clothes to her request to hand-paint napkin rings your favorite shade of blue, your mother's got a million ideas guaranteed to make your wedding day special.

While you probably won't know what to say about Mom's contributions, your fiancée, no doubt, has a few choice words. Petty conflicts can therefore arise at a time when your energy would be better spent tackling real problems. So you and your fiancée may want to think twice before you engage in a battle with your mother. Telling Mom she can't do something she really, really, *really* wants to do is a necessary evil if you want your ceremony to be respectable, right? Well, no, probably not. How horrible would it be if your mother, or anybody else involved in the ceremony, were allowed to do or make something special for you in celebration of your wedding? As long as it's not giving your guests individual photos of your former girlfriends, there's no harm in adding a homey touch to even the most sophisticated ceremony.

Your dad's job is to host the rehearsal dinner, and then stand where your mother tells him to stand. That's usually okay with him; as long as he doesn't have to get too involved, he's perfectly happy to show up and look proud. He's also there to help calm your mother when she's told that nobody wants to hear her opinion on the centerpieces, and to bail you out if you need more money than your fiancée's parents are willing to give. The perfect father of the groom is a calming influence on everyone—a sounding board for anyone in hysterics, a mature, reasonable presence at the bachelor party, and a source of solid advice for you.

Then again, the perfect mother of the groom is patient, reasonable, and reliable, but that's no guarantee that's the family you have. You'll have to rely on your parents at different points throughout the process no matter how normal or nuts they are. If you think you're about ready to kill Mom and Dad because they're being difficult, take a deep breath and mentally project yourself forward until after the wedding. Now you can see that, instead of demanding monsters, your parents are the same old lovable, slightly irritating people they always were. That feels better, doesn't it?

· Hers ·

DIVORCED PARENTS

MOST of my friends whose parents are divorced recall breathing a sigh of relief when the split happened. "Once my parents are living in different states, at least they'll stop fighting," they thought. But the momentous events of life—like a high school or college graduation and, obviously, a wedding—bring estranged parents back under the same roof, at least for a few hours. Whether the divorce was amicable or bitter, tension is bound to arise from such a reunion.

Wedding crises involving divorced parents tend to surface at similar points. Here are some typical trouble spots:

1. Who escorts the bride down the aisle. In most Christian-based ceremonies, the bride's father walks her down the aisle. Many couples follow the Jewish tradition of having both parents escort both the bride and the groom. This means you may end up walking down the aisle sandwiched between your divorced parents and praying they will behave themselves. If, God forbid, you are close to a stepparent and want him or her to walk you down the aisle, be prepared for one of your birth parents to object.

2. *Who gives the bride away.* Brrrr. Just writing those words brings me back to the nightmare of this issue at my own wedding. If there is some question as to who will give you away, you'll come to understand that *what you want doesn't matter.* Are you a full grown woman who doesn't want to be given away by anyone? Can't understand why your father alone should give you away when it took both a mother and father to raise you? Stunned by your parents' refusal to forget they are divorced for the two seconds it will take them to say, "We both do?" or for your father to say, "Her mother and I do?" Tough noogies. Who cares how you feel? It's only your wedding; it's their two seconds.

3. *Who sits where during the ceremony.* If both parents are friendly and neither is remarried, they may sit together in the first pew. If there's tension between them and one or the other has remarried, bridal etiquette books say you should seat the parent who raised you and his/her spouse in the first pew, your other parent and his/her spouse in the third pew. If this actually works for you in real life, drop me a note. I'll bake you a batch of chocolate chip cookies.

4. *Who sits where during the reception.* Dealing with this is similar to taking a four-hour drive in a Volkswagon Beetle with a Siamese and a Rottweiler running loose in the car. Don't even consider seating divorced parents at the same table. Assign them, along with their friends, to separate tables, as far apart as possible. Waving distance may be too close.

5. *Who is photographed with whom.* Each divorced parent will probably want a photograph of you with that parent, either alone or with his or her new spouse. You may want a picture of you with both your birth parents. Either way, prepare everyone ahead of time so there will be no hissy fits during photo time. Make a list that details the permutations of every desired parental shot, and walk your photographer through the list when all parties are present so he or she can make a visual ID of everyone.

6. *Who stands where in the receiving line.* Imagine standing for forty-five minutes in high heels, a corset, and ten pounds of satin and lace, being bearhugged by people you've never seen before, smiling until your face feels like it's going to fall off, wiping away a hundred lipstick kisses, while your mother and father trade insults over your head. Doesn't sound like a picnic?

The good news is, traditionally fathers don't have to stand in the receiving line, so your mother can be content to give him the hairy eyeball from across the room while she receives the guests alone. If you want your father in the receiving line, don't position him next to your mother, or yourself between the two of them.

The last thing you want to deal with during the planning process or on your wedding day itself is the fallout from someone else's failed marriage. So to ease stress and sidestep problems, you'll need a plan. Some guidelines:

- *Determine early on who will pay for what.* Dividing up the budget may be a big source of conflict for divorced parents, in that there may be arguments over who's paying the bigger share and who's not fulfilling whose parental responsibilities. Try to arbitrate the financial struggle without getting involved in the emotional one. Start by telling your parents how important your wedding is to you and that you appreciate whatever financial help they can give you in order to make it a great day.

- *Include both parents equally.* Keep them involved and informed, so neither feels left out. If one or both parents have remarried, you need to be sensitive to their feelings. If you've developed a close relationship with your stepmother, for example, you'll have to consciously include your own mother equally.

- *Don't take it personally.* As hard as your parents' divorce was on you, imagine how tough it was on the two of them. They may easily become so wrapped up in their own unpleasant feelings that they forget this is supposed to be your day. Having experienced the dissolution of a marriage, they might lack the optimism you feel going into your own. One bride told me her father kept trying to talk her out of getting married throughout the planning process, and even whispered, "It's not too late to call it off" as they walked down the aisle. Just remember, you are not your parents. Their problems are not your problems, and you're entitled to fully enjoy your wedding and the marriage that follows.

· His ·

DIVORCED PARENTS

WHY do so many divorced parents act like children when their sons or daughters get married? Perhaps your wedding brings back unpleasant memories of a very difficult time for them. Maybe the divorce wasn't amicable or they're still dealing with unresolved emotional issues, and they hate the thought of interacting with their ex as anything other than plaintiff and defendant. Or there's the possibility that *you're* so wrapped up in your own wedding plans that you haven't had the time or energy to concentrate on making them happy (imagine that!).

Regardless, everything you need to know about dealing with divorced parents before your wedding you learned in kindergarten.

- To avoid unruly fathers and stepfathers throwing punches at each other, keep them separated, each one facing a corner.

- "I don't care what Dad's 'trampy' wife is wearing, Mother, you are not leaving this house without a bra!"

- There will be no crying or whining in the church. The golden rule is: Nobody gives anybody away.

- "No, Dad, we didn't invite any 'eligible babes.'"

- Parents with a problem should sit quietly until called upon.

- "You will stand next to your ex-husband in the receiving line and *you will like it!*"

- Good parents never threaten to withhold money when they don't get their way, unless they can spell e-l-o-p-e.

- "There are desperate fathers in China who would love to dance with their ex-wives, now shut up and waltz."

- Daddies who can't behave themselves in front of mommies are welcome to leave the party.

- "Would you like to share your nasty little affair with the rest of the family? Then perhaps you should do what you're told."

- Everyone loves a smiling parent. The reward for pouting is a one-way ticket to Mopeyville.

- "Whose wedding is it? That's right, boys and girls, it's *my* wedding."

If your parents are divorced, they may be reluctant to plan an elaborate event such as a rehearsal dinner together. Sticky issues will arise, like who pays for what and who receives a prominent role in the ceremony. The last thing you need on your wedding day is to baby-sit your parents. Hopefully, they will have the presence of mind and the graciousness to put aside their personal differences and allow you and your fiancée to enjoy your day to the fullest.

Unfortunately, that doesn't usually happen without effort on your part. Engaged couples with one or two sets of divorced parents often face the added burden of helping everyone feel more comfortable throughout the wedding. You can do this through any of the following: open discussions with all the natural mothers and fathers, exes, and steppeople involved; seating and receiving line arrangements that keep incompatible parents apart; the assignment of equal ceremony roles to those who put forth equal effort to raise you or your fiancée; and encouraging each parent to communicate freely with the others. What you *don't* want is to be stuck in the middle of negotiations or disputes. You're the groom, not the town sheriff, and any parent who tries to treat you like an arbitrator should be told in no uncertain terms to deal with it him- or herself.

A family is forced to suffer through many difficult emotions when put through a divorce, but not one of those emotions has any place at a wedding. Crying, yes. Anger, no. Happiness, yes. Bitterness, no. Bliss, yes. Blame, no. If you or your wife was a child of divorce, you probably always wished for the one thing you couldn't have: a happy, functional home life. A wonderful wedding gift would be for your parents to create that illusion for one special day.

·Hers·

BEST MAN AND GROOMSMEN

A great deal is riding upon your husband's choice of attendants. In his reception toast, for example, a well-chosen best man will give a heartfelt speech about his relationship with the groom and the joy of your union, whereas a poor choice of a best man will depict your husband as the one-time Casanova of Michigan U., congratulate you on having "caught" him, and remind you that all those chicks whose hearts he's broken are still waiting in the wings.

A considerate best man will organize a bachelor party for your fiancé that doesn't involve you cleaning up any sort of body fluid the next morning. He'll show up at the wedding early, and he'll remember what your parents look like in order to properly escort them down the aisle. A "lemon" of a best man will dump your fiancé on your doorstep after the bachelor party with a DO NOT DISTURB sign taped to his face.

While personality is less important in the groomsmen and ushers than in the best man, it's helpful if these people can be made serviceably attractive without the help of a full-body shave. The last thing you want to deal with is your bridesmaids fighting over who has to walk down the aisle with the usher who looks like Quasimodo, and we all know how the pictures turn out when you've got to match your escorts with everyone from Stretch McGee to Wee Willy.

Unfortunately, you don't have a lot of say in the matter when it comes to your husband's selection of his half of the wedding party. If you have a brother or male best friend, you may suggest that one or both of them be included as ushers. Other than that, it's your fiancé's call, and whatever makes him happy goes. All you can do is make sure it's the most well-behaved one of the bunch who's escorting your three eldest aunties down the aisle.

> ### SEVEN SURVIVAL TIPS FOR GETTING ALONG WITH GROOMSMEN
>
> 1. Drink an entire beer through your nose.
> 2. Tell them you'll be out of town the weekend of the bachelor party.
> 3. First one to shave gets his pick of the bridesmaids.
> 4. Chat with them when they call.
> 5. Don't beat them at games—especially poker.
> 6. Act like you understand why they choose to watch golf.
> 7. Show more cleavage.

It's a smart idea to start kissing up to the whole crew of groomsmen a good five months before the wedding. Go ahead, pour it on. Make them love you. Suggest that the boys take a few nights each week to hang out without any women involved, go to a few bars, have a few beers . . . they deserve some all-guy time together.

In return, all you ask is for them to plan the bachelor party well before the wedding—preferably weeks or months, not days. It's one thing to deal with a hungover worthless fiancé for a weekend when there's nothing on the agenda except planning some last wedding-related details. It's a whole different ballgame to end up like Brenda. She didn't know that a merry band of ushers/cavemen had thrown the bachelor party for Jerry, her fiancé, the night before the wedding. She learned this for the first time when, after consuming his weight in Absolut a mere twelve hours previously, Jerry stood at the altar trembling at the sight of his bride resplendently marching down the aisle, then vomited all over his shiny rented shoes.

· *His* ·

BEST MAN AND GROOMSMEN

IF you have a brother you like, your best man decision should be easy. If you have several brothers, or if you hate your brother's guts, your choice gets substantially more difficult.

One family of four brothers laid out a foolproof best man plan when they were in their early teens. No matter where or when their weddings occurred, no matter who was angry at whom, they would forget their differences and, in order of birth, brother #2 would be best man to brother #1, #3 to #2, #4 to #3, and #1 to #4. This arrangement worked pretty well, because when the older brothers were ready to get married, their best men were older than twenty-one, and therefore legally able to arrange for the alcohol and live entertainment required at the bachelor party.

Grooms without brothers have a few options to choose from. One choice is to have your father as best man. Often this is an honorary title, since father of the groom is a job in itself, and most dads have little interest in arranging a bachelor party so they can see their sons passed out on the floor of a strip bar. Another option is to make your fiancée's brother the best man—which scores points with her family but does little to endear you to your friends. Finally, you can appoint your best friend as best man—which brings you to the fun task of deciding which of your friends is your *best* friend.

Sometimes it's obvious, like the guy you've known since first grade, or your college roommate for all four years. Sometimes you have to go with your gut, or ask yourself who you think would do the best job. If you can't pick one friend without alienating the others, it's perfectly acceptable to make them all best men—or not have one at all. Put one groomsman in charge of the bachelor party, another in charge of holding the rings at the ceremony, a third in charge of paying the officiant, and assign the whole group the responsibility for the toast.

As a rule, guys aren't likely to get jealous and huffy if you don't ask them to be in your wedding. Still, in the case of people who have asked you to be a groomsman or usher at their wedding, there may be some hard feelings if you don't return the gesture. Fortunately, nobody ever said there was a limit to the number or the gender of the people you can put in your wedding party. You can invite your whole circle of friends, men and women, to take the plunge with you, and if your fiancée's side of the aisle is stocked with fewer people, lend her some of yours. Think of your wedding as the biggest party you've ever thrown for all of the people you love most, not as a homecoming dance where there is a king, a queen, and a limited hierarchy of dignitaries. If your friends and family don't fit into the traditional structure of wedding parties, then bend or break the tradition.

Now, once you've chosen your best man and groomsmen (and your fiancée agrees—an important step, to be skipped at your peril) you have to formally ask these people to be a part of your big day. Doing so in person is usually best, maybe over a meal or a beer. Give them as much warning as possible so they can keep your wedding date free on their calendars, and give them a range of what this might mean to them financially—$100 for tuxedos, say, $150 for a hotel room, and who knows what for the bachelor party. Or, if you're feeling flush, offer to pay their expenses yourself. Keep in mind that you are telling these men how special they are to you, so treat asking them to be in your wedding like the honor that it is.

Finally, to thank your groomsmen for their extra efforts on and before your wedding day, you'll need to buy each member of your wedding party a gift, which is traditionally distributed at the rehearsal dinner. For economy's sake, it makes sense to buy each person the same gift, preferably monogrammed with his initials.

Try to come up with something more creative than a tie or a pocket knife. Think, what do all these guys have in common? Do we love baseball? Do we love beer? Are we all synchronized swimmers? Give something relevant to everyone that's cool and a little bit unexpected, but don't go overboard on the price. And no matter what you give, don't expect it to be proudly displayed in your friend's home when you come over after the wedding. I mean, you're a great pal and all, but there's not a lot of day-to-day use for a life-size bobbing-head Orioles doll with your buddy's name printed on the jersey.

· Hers ·

MAID OF HONOR AND BRIDESMAIDS

WHEN selecting your bridesmaids, there are two patches of landmine-seeded ground over which you'll likely have to travel. You'll see the first one coming from miles away; in fact, mere hours after becoming engaged you'll probably start wracking your brain to determine who you're obligated to have in your wedding party versus who you'd *like* to have in your wedding party.

Start by considering how many total bridesmaids you see yourself having in an ideal world. Do you want only your two closest friends, or an entourage swathed in taffeta? Once you've arrived at a number, start sifting through your relatives. Sisters, close cousins, single Aunt Margaret. Then consider your fiancé's family. If he has sisters, are you close to them? Are you obligated to include them as bridesmaids anyway? Now think back to every wedding you've been in. Which of those brides are you still good friends with? Who would be likely to put a hex on you if you didn't reciprocate and ask her to be a bridesmaid at your wedding?

With the obligatory slots filled in, you're free to select the rest of your bridesmaids based on your personal wishes. It helps to make your choices with the goal of achieving a balanced mix of personalities. Every bridal party needs a good Organizer, for instance. Who else is going to throw you the perfect bridal shower and make sure everyone knows where you're registered? To complement the Organizer, every bridal party needs a Fun Person. The Organizer will swing into immediate helpful action if you decide, insanely, to change the bridesmaids' dresses two weeks before the wedding, but the Fun Person will crack jokes at your expense until you realize what an overwrought jerk you're being. You'll also need an Emoter to calm your nerves and empathize with your crazy mood swings, sudden tantrums, and crying jags, and finally, a good Listener who will allow you to complain about the same subject for a solid year.

The second landmine is that, inevitably, people will be unhappy with your bridal party selection. Your mother will complain because you've chosen people of all different heights and weights, which will keep the pictures from being perfect. Your ultratraditional grandmother will blow a gasket when she learns you've also asked your best friend Charles to be on your side of the wedding party. Like the forgotten fairy at Sleeping Beauty's christening, some poor overlooked friend will tell you at the last minute that she wishes you all the best, but she's hurt that you clearly don't value her friendship as much as she values yours and she's therefore boycotting the wedding.

Since everyone has forgotten the significance of having bridesmaids in the first place (it involved an ancient Celtic ritual of surrounding the bride with guardians because a crowd of men, including the groom, would traditionally try to kidnap her the night before the wedding), these days the purpose of the wedding party is to keep you happy and stable before and during the big day. It is the duty of the bridesmaids to remain enthusiastic, interested, and supportive of your wedding plans long after everyone else around you is bored stiff of hearing about hors d'oeuvres and dyed satin pumps.

So don't be afraid to be selfish with your selection. If your grade school friend Ermintrude invited you to be in her wedding but she's the kind of high-strung person who's fun to be around for about thirty seconds, then trust me, you don't want her in your wedding party. Find a way to graciously mention that you were honored by the opportunity to be her bridesmaid and you value your relationship with her, but you won't be able to ask her to be an attendant. There are good reasons and bad reasons to not include a friend in your wedding party. The fact that she's overweight and won't look good in the dress of your dreams is a bad reason. The fact that she's due to give birth the same day as your wedding, well, that kind of double-booking has disaster written all over it.

Finally, be prepared for the occasional friend to decline your offer to be a bridesmaid. Sometimes even your closest friends can be too cash-strapped or wedding-weary to be supportive members of your wedding party. It may seem that someone who backs out of your wedding is effectively putting a price on the friendship, but at least in the end, only those who really want to be in your wedding will be there with you.

MAID OF HONOR AND BRIDESMAIDS

BEHIND every successful wedding, there's a capable crew of women who make things happen. They calm your fiancée when you can't, they shower her with support and praise, they advise her on her makeup, hairstyle, and dress, and, most delightfully of all, they tell you to get the hell out of the way. In the end, you're just a pawn in their matrimonial game. You can accept your position on the board, or fight it at your own peril.

My suggestion? As long as the bridesmaids make your fiancée happy, give them all the power they want. They are far too important in the wedding-planning process for you to alienate them. Just make sure you have the right number of groomsmen and ushers to escort each of them down the aisle. If you have to cut on your side, give your extra friends some other job to do, like reading a poem or lighting candles.

At some point, you and your fiancée will have to decide which of your groomsmen will be paired up with which of her bridesmaids during the ceremony. In order to make this decision scientifically, let's examine the cast of female characters you're likely to be faced with:

The Maid of Evil—uh, Honor. Typically your fiancée's sister and polar opposite. Though I had no objection to my sister-in-law, I've heard stories of many who styled themselves after the Wicked Witch of the West. She knows everything about you (via your wife), and she's willing to use the most sensitive information for emotional gain. Your greatest satisfaction will be pairing her up with your best man, the college friend you could always count on to say the entire alphabet within a single burp.

The Bitter Spinster. As usual, she's a bridesmaid again, and from the looks of that sour puss, there's no sign of a husband on the horizon. When it's time to walk down the aisle, stick her with the biggest Romeo among your groomsmen and see if he can fry her bacon.

The Power Broker. Stick-thin and smartly dressed, she'll take over the bridal shower, offer suggestions to the photographer, rearrange all the flowers, and tell you exactly where to stand. You'd love to tell her where to get off. Instead, saddle her with your biggest pothead usher, then watch her drag him down the aisle by his droopy eyelids.

The Flower Child. A vegan hippy-chick with unshaven legs and Stevie Nicks hair. Probably the coolest of all your wife's friends...and the least reliable. Your youngest brother is the perfect match for her. He'll think she's funky and she'll think he's cute.

The Moon Unit. What's she saying? Nobody knows, but she'll go on for hours about it. The only thing more astonishing than her brainless logic is her unerring ability to lock her keys in her car. Make sure your most buttoned-up groomsman is responsible for getting her to the church on time and preventing her from attempting to think.

No matter what combination of characters you're faced with, try hard to strike up a friendly relationship with them. Not only will they be an important part of your wedding, they'll likely be main characters in the rest of your life. There's no better time than the present to lay the groundwork for an amicable relationship with your new wife's friends.

MALE ATTIRE

My sister learned a valuable life lesson when her senior prom date showed up in a white tuxedo with a gold sequined bow tie and cummerbund: Never let a man you will be seen with in public pick out his own clothes. While this is a useful philosophy, putting it into practice by helping your husband select his wedding attire and that of his groomsmen and ushers can be a tricky business. Even men who don't profess strong feelings about any other element of the wedding and reception want to be able to dress themselves without anyone's help on the day they get married. You must guide them gently toward the right decision, all the while supporting their belief that the formalwear choice was completely their own.

Have you heard of the communication technique called "mirroring"? This is where you listen, nonjudgmentally, to what your partner says, then paraphrase it back so that he knows you've heard him. An example might be when your fiancé says, "I'm going to pick out my tuxedo today," and you say, "What I hear is that you're going to pick out your tuxedo today." By using a slight variation on the mirroring technique, you can convince your fiancé that he's thought and said what you *want* him to think and say, rather than what came out of his mouth. So, to the words "I'm going to pick out my tuxedo today," you respond,

"What I hear is that you'd like me to help you pick out your tuxedo today."

Here's some more psychological trickery to use when the two of you are actually in the tuxedo store:

1. *Positive reinforcement.* Lavish praise on your fiancé's correct choices and remain stone-faced and mute about his bad choices. Make your fiancé beg for your opinion: "No, honey, this is your choice, and I wouldn't dream of influencing your decision by telling you what people will say if you come down the aisle wearing—that."

2. *Bribery.* Slip the salesman a twenty (happens to him all the time) and teach him some simple cues. Thumbs-up means he should ooh and aah; thumbs-down means he should clear his throat and say, "I'm afraid this one makes you look a bit... scrawny and wimpish. Shall we try another?"

3. *The old switcheroo.* While your fiancé is parading around the shop in his skivvies, load up the dressing room with your selections and return his choices to the rack. Don't worry about detection. The extent of his internal dialogue will be, "I don't really remember it, but I guess I must have picked this one out since it's here in the dressing room."

This isn't to say that there aren't men with impeccable taste; men who have stronger opinions than you do when it comes to registering for china and designing your invitations. These guys can carry off a sunflower-printed vest under their morning suit and don't need or want a word of feedback from you. But for most people, the only way to know what looks best on them is to actually see it on their body, and this runs counterintuitive to the way men shop. Men generally don't believe that the personality of the wearer affects the look of a garment, and they will never understand the concept of trying things on.

A guy will go into a store, see something on the rack, and say, "Looks good, I'll take it." The way to break down this wall of resistance is to make comments like, "I bet you'll look so hot in this tux that I'm going to want to rip it off you right here in the middle of the mall." Then, when he tries it on, say, "Nah, I was wrong. You look like a potato. Now *this* one *here* will really get my motor running." Keep this up and you may get him to try on every suit in the store.

· *His* ·

MALE ATTIRE

IF there's one day when you want to look well dressed, it's your wedding. And not just well dressed according to your own standards, either. You want everyone in the room, including your aunt, the famous designer, to look at you and think "Zowie! He looks sharp!" Your usual daily fashion safety check ("Does it clash? No. Is it zipped? Yes. Does it itch? No.") is only a starting point when it comes to selecting wedding attire.

But unless you're a regular reader of men's fashion magazines or you've spent time working in high-end apparel, you will most likely be out of your league the minute you walk into a tuxedo shop. Fortunately, most tuxedo salespeople know this and they're happy to point out something that, literally, suits you. When you go in to scope out the range of possible outfits, be sure to ask a lot of questions. Use words like "classic," "designer," and "top-of-the-line-but-not-too-expensive." Avoid words like "ruffles," "maroon," and "factory seconds." Better yet, bring your fiancée with you and let her do the talking. Luckily, there's no superstition about seeing the groom all dressed up before the wedding.

In fact, bring your mother along. Bring her mother, too. You see, trying on tuxedos isn't like trying on jeans at the mall. When you come out of that dressing room decked out in a forty-long Armani, women will stare at you like you're Brad Pitt. Whether or not you've brought your own personal female audience, women will gather around: saleswomen, other guys' fiancées, passers-by. They'll hoot. They'll holler. They'll pull on lapels and check cuffs. The only difference between this and a crowd at Chippendale's is that they won't be yelling "Take it off!" After all, it probably took them twenty or thirty years to get you *in* the damn thing. I suggest you enjoy the attention.

As you're considering different tuxedo styles, remember that your groomsmen have to rent the same thing you do. That's in addition to the gifts they're buying you, the bachelor party they're throwing, and possibly the overnight hotel stay they're footing the bill for on the weekend of your wedding. While the Porsche of tuxedoes may be the nicest one in the store, you may want to settle for a sporty little Miata so that your friends won't have to take out second mortgages to be in your wedding. Tread lightly on their wallets in the formalwear department and they'll thank you later by not making you pay an arm and a leg to be in their weddings.

Once you've settled on your tuxedo style and had your measurements taken, all you have to do is maintain your weight for your wedding. That's easy enough to say, but more than one groom has dealt with prewedding

SEVEN SURVIVAL TIPS FOR CHOOSING TUXEDOS WITH YOUR FIANCÉE

1. Agree in advance on a reasonable price limit based on the resources of your groomsmen.
2. Let your fiancée go into the tuxedo store first, while you make sure everything's copacetic at the food court.
3. Jumping out of the dressing room wearing a pale blue top hat and tails is funny only to you.
4. Lose weight before you go if you don't want to be poked in the belly and called "Pork Chop."
5. Make sure you're wearing underwear with no holes or little duckies.
6. Make sure you wear underwear.
7. Two words are a husband's best friend: "Yes, dear."

nerves by consuming a daily dose of deep-dish pizza with extra cheese. If the big day arrives and you find out your tuxedo is five pounds smaller than you are, follow this instant weight-loss plan:

1. consume your body weight in water, and

2. pee like you've never peed before.

· Hers ·

BRIDESMAIDS' DRESSES

YOU'VE probably already heard every bridesmaid's dress joke in the book. Nope, cancel that. You've probably *seen* every bridesmaid's dress joke in the book. This is because many of these getups are hilarious-looking no matter how hard the bride tries to be tasteful, diplomatic, and unique. It's impossible to escape the Paradox of the Bridesmaid's Dress: you're bound for failure if you try to find one outfit that universally flatters a batch of bridesmaids of varying heights, weights, and complexions.

Let's take a case study. Monica had five bridesmaids:

Joelle, 5'7", 125 lbs.; blond hair; size 6

Sandra, 5'5", 135 lbs.; red hair; size 8

Denise, 5'6", 175 lbs.; blond hair; size 16

Patty, 5'10", 120 lbs.; brunette; size 0

Mindy, 5', 105 lbs., brunette; size 2

Patty was skinny, Sandra was busty, and Joelle would be seven months pregnant at the time of the wedding. At first, Monica thought the solution would be to simply tell these very differently shaped women to go out and buy a formal dress that they felt comfortable in. After all, bridesmaids aren't sheep, so why should they be dressed in identical outfits, with identical shoes and identical flowers in their identically styled hair?

While this plan made perfect sense to Monica, her mother wouldn't hear of it. She insisted that Monica pick out one dress style and have it shipped, in the appropriate size, to each bridesmaid. Monica did so, but when her mother-in-law-to-be saw the dress, she pitched a fit. The chosen dress was apparently the wrong style, the wrong color, the wrong fabric, and made by the wrong designer. Monica gave up and turned over the dress selection to her future mother-in-law, which completely irritated her mother.

As if that weren't enough to contend with, Monica's mother-in-law refused to select the dress without seeing each bridesmaid try it on in person. The maid of honor, Denise, had given birth only a few months before and wouldn't go into a dressing room until she had lost "enough" weight. That didn't happen until a mere four weeks before the wedding. Luckily, the mother-in-law pulled some strings at a fancy bridal store and the dresses were ready in time, but Monica was so stressed out and angry over this issue that she literally lost her voice.

So how can you avoid this nightmare? Well, for one, if you're not a believer in cookie-cutter bridesmaids' dresses, insist on your rights. Try to find some compromises. Go to a mid- or upscale department store where they stock dresses fancy enough for the wedding party without being prom-like, and ask for a range of sizes. Or order a specific fabric and then allow each bridesmaid to have a dress made out of it. You can achieve some photogenic uniformity by suggesting that all the dresses be, for example, sleeveless and ankle-length.

If, on the other hand, you want all your bridesmaids dressed exactly alike, make it as easy for them as possible. Get their measurements and order all the dresses. Order their shoes, their jewelry, and their stockings. If it's important to you, go the extra mile and don't leave it up to chance. And remember, no detail is too small. If you're the type who will freak out when a bridesmaid arrives dressed exactly as planned but with her nails painted Harlot Red, then make sure you specify ahead of time what color nail polish is acceptable and what isn't.

Money could be an issue for your bridesmaids; if they've already been in four weddings this year, at approximately three hundred a pop for brides-maid's gear, your selection may be the last straw that will send them into bankruptcy. Even if cost isn't an issue or if they're too shy to complain about it, it's a nice gesture for you to pick up some of the expenses of your brides-maids' attire. Then again, there's only so much you can cover. Many of these same women will probably expect you to buy your own bridesmaid's accou-trements for their weddings, if you haven't done so already. Try to give your attendants fair warning of the costs your wedding will engender (better yet, get your maid of honor to do it), so that they can start saving up for your big day.

If the thought of doing all the dress shopping yourself makes you break out in hives, set priorities and let go of the thought that all the accessories have to match. You can focus on the dress, and let your bridesmaids pick out stock-ings and any style shoe in the basic color you suggest. And for heaven's sake, pick a dress that's easy to wear. Even if you have the figure of a fashion model, your bridesmaids may not, so don't make everybody wear some slinky Gaultier knock-off. One bride, Arlene, learned this the hard way. Her brides-maids organized a full-out mutiny against the clingy sheath she'd chosen, so Arlene had to return everything long distance, then start over from scratch.

Want to cut off any potential rebellion at the pass? Use my favorite dress story as a guide. Ellen continually sent her bridesmaids pictures of the ugliest outfits she could find — the best was turquoise harem pants with a hot pink silk blouse. The bridesmaids couldn't have been happier or more grateful when they were told what the final choice would be — basic black.

· *His* ·

BRIDESMAIDS' DRESSES

I know what you're thinking. Why should you care what the bridesmaids wear, and what in the world could possibly make this your problem? Well, when the woman you love cries hysterically, throws coffee mugs through the living room window, and slams the phone down so hard it comes off the wall, it's your problem. Dealing with bridesmaids' dresses will make your fiancée do all of these things sooner or later, so you'd better prepare for the onslaught now.

First, you will be asked what you think of various fabrics, colors, and styles. Getting through this level of hell will require words like "cheery," "slimming," "vibrant," "versatile," and "flattering." When asked for your opinion on the physical attributes of the fine women your fiancée has assembled for her wedding party, stick with "natural," "youthful," "perky," "bright," and "not nearly as beautiful as you, honey." Words to stay away from are "barfy," "frightening," "beached whale," "boring," and "wow, look at those hooters."

In all seriousness, selection of the bridesmaids' dresses, gargantuan and iridescent as they may be, is a matter of grave importance to your future wife.

So you should treat it as such, at least when you're around her. Even though you know that when the wedding is over everyone will laugh about the problems these dresses caused, it's no laughing matter now. Above all your fiancée needs your support. Give it to her, unconditionally. And stand by her side when the harpies start shrieking about their dresses.

Of course, when the lovely ladies-in-waiting stop screaming, they'll be fishing for compliments from you about their attire (though they won't really care to hear your opinion). Here's a helpful list of bridesmaid-specific praises that are sure to please. Feel free to use them. No extra charge.

"Honey, you put the yow in yowza."

"I'm sorry, miss, there's no smoking in here." *Probable response:* "But I'm not smoking." *Proper bon mot:* "Oh yes... you are."

"I had no idea Gwyneth Paltrow was invited to our wedding."

"That dress makes you look ten years younger. What are you really, twenty-three?"

"Do you look fat? My god, woman, I could lift you with my pinky."

"You are gonna be one heck of a target for that bouquet."

"You just say the word and we'll make this a two-bride wedding."

· *Hers* ·

THE WEDDING DRESS

As women aged five to one hundred, our wedding fantasies begin and end with the Dress. We picture heads turning as we walk down the aisle in—the Dress. We imagine lovingly drying the tears our mother sheds in the dressing room, gazing upon us wearing—the Dress. We rehearse in our minds the moment when the groom waiting at the altar catches his first glimpse of us in—the Dress. For years after the wedding, we know, our friends and family members will comment upon our exquisite taste in selecting—the Dress.

No bride before us has ever had, and no bride after us will ever have, a dress to compare. We pore through issue after issue of *Modern Bride*, and a recurring thought goes through our heads: "Princess Diana's dress was nice, but it has nothing on mine." At every wedding we attend, we think either "My dress will be better" or "My dress had hers beat all to hell." You can capitalize the Little Black Dress if you want to, but one of life's great truths is that there's only one dress deserving of such punctuation and that's the Big White One.

What all this adds up to is that soon you'll be looking for: one, a dress you've been waiting your whole life to buy, and two, a dress that has to be better than any other dress worn by any other bride ever. And you've got how many months to find it? In every wedding there's one aspect of the planning that spirals out of control, becoming bizarrely difficult. For some couples it's the invitations, or the seating arrangements, or the favors. But in many weddings, the most difficult part—for both the bride and the groom, who must be supportive of her—turns out to be buying the wedding dress.

For most women, this seems ironic, since wedding-dress shopping involves going shopping, spending lots and lots of money, being the center of attention, and having a record number of people tell you you're beautiful. But my own experience bears this out: the selection of my wedding dress was so traumatic that Dave practically had to tie me to the desk to get me to write about it. At the end of an intensive six-month search, during which I dragged every person I've ever been remotely friendly with into dressing rooms across the country, I had purchased two dresses I felt were unwearable. So twenty-four hours before the wedding, I was fitted for the rental dress in which I was actually married.

Finding the dress is hard enough, but first you have to decide who to find the dress with. Paulette's friends had warned her against shopping with her mother, saying that mothers have their own issues and a wedding dress is an adult purchase that you want to shop for as an adult. Regardless, Paulette went shopping with anyone who wanted to go, including her mother. Soon she realized that no matter who else was there, when she came out of the dressing room she always looked at her mom's face first. Then the nightmares began. Paulette dreamed of going dress shopping and walking into a warehouse filled with dresses, all up too high to see, only to be told that her mother had already picked out a dress for her.

In addition to worrying about whether she looked fat in white and what the dresses she tried on were "saying" about her, Paulette now worried that shopping with her mother had put a curse on the whole process. But in the end, everything worked out. Paulette says, "For me there was no moment of 'That's it, that's my dress.' I bought it because when I came out of the dressing room, my mom said, 'Now there's a wedding dress.' She was right. Plus she ended up negotiating a much better deal than I could have alone."

The selection of a wedding dress doesn't have to be so traumatic. Here are some tips that may make the process easier, both emotionally and logistically.

1. *List your personal likes and dislikes.* If you have always disliked showing cleavage, you're not going to like it any more on your wedding day. Do some soul searching to come up with a list of things you need and want: "I hate cleavage. I love lace. I prefer long sleeves and off-the-shoulder to sleeveless or v-necked."

2. *Narrow your options.* Wedding dress shopping can feel overwhelming just because of the sheer number of choices. When you've looked at dresses in a thousand bridal stores, there are still a thousand more stores to look at and a new issue of *Bride's* coming out with a passel of next season's dresses. Use the list you just made to create guidelines that narrow down your choices. Follow the guidelines strictly when you shop: "I only want to look at off-white. I only want to look at dresses in this price range."

3. *Focus on your #1 priority.* There are three key components in wedding dress shopping: what the dress looks like, how much it costs, and where you buy it. Which is most important to you? Maureen's dress shopping became infinitely easier when she realized the place to buy the dress was more important to her than the dress itself. She'd been to the wedding superstores; the sample sales; the "running of the bulls" events where expensive stores get rid of their overstock in a few frenzied sale hours. Then she found a shop where the salespeople offered her a glass of wine while bringing out one pre-selected dress at a time, and she stopped looking anywhere else.

4. *Educate yourself.* Read magazines, try on dresses, look at your friends' wedding gowns. You've had your entire life to learn how to dress yourself for everyday, but suddenly you have less than a year to learn how to attire yourself in a giant white dress. Put yourself on a crash course to accelerate the learning curve.

5. *Find one person to trust.* Dress selection can mushroom into such a life-or-death scenario that you'll be tempted to solicit the opinions of anyone and everyone you know. But this is a decision that doesn't need to be made by committee. My friend Laura picked out a dress while on a business trip and asked one acquaintance on the trip to give her a second opinion. All she needed was a

little objective feedback to confirm her own feelings. That's all you need, too — whether that feedback comes from your mother, your best friend, your fiancé, a respected colleague, or a salesperson whom you've come to trust.

6. *Don't get sucked into prevailing fashion trends.* When you look at your wedding pictures in twenty years, you don't want to be embarrassed that you chose something that wasn't you. You'd rather your kids said, "Wow!" than, "Mom, what were you thinking?" There's no need to go for the big-bow-on-the-butt look or a Prada-esque silk shift if these aren't the styles you already wear instinctively. You'll see dresses that look like unmade beds, and dresses that seem designed to make your butt appear as big as possible. You'll be surrounded by sycophantic salespeople whose job is to convince you that everything you put on looks absolutely perfect. Be strong.

7. *Consider alternatives.* A woman's wedding attire used to be restricted to white, pearls, and pumps. But brides have come to realize that you can be elegant and formal without the usual big skirt and beaded train; you can look every bit as much a bride in a celery-colored dress as a white one, or in your mother's dress remade to fit you instead of the newest, most expensive make and model.

8. *Make your own rules.* "Don't wear a necklace with a tiara or jeweled headpiece," the wedding magazines say. "Don't wear flats if you're under five-eight." Who cares? If you like glitz and glitter, no one should convince you to tone it down. If you like things plain, don't listen to anyone who says you need decoration in order to look bridal. What's more important, using high heels to "balance the fullness of your skirt" or being able to dance and circulate among your guests in shoes you find comfortable?

9. *Good is good enough.* For months after my wedding I kept buying wedding magazines and seeing new dresses, thinking, "Oh, if only I'd tried on that one," or "Now that really would have been perfect." Even if you never get hit over the head with the "Oh, my god, this is my dress" feeling; even if your budget limits your search to dresses that aren't quite the stuff of your dreams; even if you change your mind about liking your dress three hours before the wedding; you will be a beautiful bride. There never has been, and never will be, a bride who doesn't glow on her wedding day. A little lace and some rhinestones will never change that.

· *His* ·

THE WEDDING DRESS

BEING a man has many advantages, foremost of which is that we never have to ask anyone if we're fat. We know we're fat, because we stopped exercising three months into our gym membership and we consume three pints of Ben & Jerry's Chunky Monkey (soon to be Chubby Hubby) every week. It's obvious when we look in the mirror that a spare tire is developing around our middles, but through the inequities of society, this revelation does not deeply affect our self-esteem.

As you know, your fiancée is wired differently. Chances are, her body image has a lot to do with her moods, her confidence level, and her choice of clothing. Which brings us to the wedding dress, arguably the most important, angst-ridden clothing choice she'll ever make. If you're very lucky, your fiancée will consult her mother, a dress store owner, and perhaps a dress designer, make a decision, stick with it, and the first time you'll even think about the dress is when you see her wearing it as she walks down the aisle toward you. If your situation is more typical, you'll have to get involved.

For most grooms, the wedding dress is the cause of quite a few specific mini dramas, and they all fall under three major categories: style, price, and weight. Here's what to expect when your fiancée tries to deal with all three.

Style. You've probably never seen a truly ugly wedding dress. Such a thing doesn't exist: they're all sort of whitish, sometimes lacy, sometimes plain. Every so often a bride goes for something wilder like a brash red or an emerald green, but chances are the color will match her personality, so no one who knows her will be embarrassed or outraged by her choice. The point is, you know that your fiancée really can't go wrong with her wedding dress, so you may wonder why finding the right one is such a big deal. Well, unless this is her second wedding, your fiancée has never worn a wedding dress before, and she feels compelled to find, on her first try, the kind of gown that says "Wow! *Here* comes the bride!"

She may ask you for your advice, something you're barely qualified to offer having presumably never worn a wedding dress yourself. She'll wonder whether you like what the bride's wearing when you go to other weddings. She'll point at dresses in shop windows and say, "Whaddya think?" She'll hand you a thousand-page bridal magazine and ask you to pick out the styles you like. As much as you would rather read just about anything else, it would only take a few minutes for you to go through and point to some dresses that look nice. Be honest, and don't get discouraged if she hates your choices. At least you're giving her some idea of what you like, and she can file that information in among the many bits of advice she'll receive from friends and relatives. Eventually, she'll put all the opinions together and make her own decision on style. Your input will help, if even in the smallest of ways.

Price. Traditionally, the bride or her family covers the cost of all her clothing. But if they set a tight budget, some or all of the costs may fall on you. Of all the components of your wedding, the dress will be the most visible, the one your wife will save for the longest time, and the item that will receive the most compliments. Skimping is not recommended. At the same time, there are thousands of styles in a reasonable price range for your bride to choose from. If she absolutely, positively must have the most expensive dress on the block, do what you can to help her afford it, whether you supplement her or her parents' contribution with your own money, or ask your parents for a little help. It's worth the extra expense for your fiancée to get exactly what she wants.

Weight. Not the weight of the dress, though it's often considerable. I'm referring to your fiancée's weight, which will affect her mood from the day she starts trying on dresses to the moment she walks down the aisle. Your duty throughout this period goes far beyond answering "No" to the question, "Do I look fat?" Your job is to assure your fiancée in every way possible that she is a beautiful, attractive woman whose weight is of absolutely no consequence to you whatsoever. Compliment her often, and do it spontaneously. Hold her and tell her she's beautiful. Support her in her quest to lose five more pounds for the sake of the dress — even if you don't think she's fat, you'll never be able to convince her of that.

Whatever you do, never tell her she has a few more to lose. Show your fiancée that you love her, and her imaginary weight problems will take care of themselves. Then go off and take care of another pint of Ben & Jerry's.

The Wedding Sketch-O-Matic

There's nothing like a pop psychology test for making a man and woman look at each other and say, "I didn't know that about you." Either that or, "That was a stupid pop psychology test." Anyway, here's an exercise that's guaranteed to make you say something to each other, good or bad. To begin, each of you get a piece of 8½-by-11-inch paper and some Magic Markers. Then follow the instructions on the list below. Be sure to finish drawing each image before you move on to the next one.

Imagine you and your future spouse are on a remote island.

Anywhere on the page, draw the house you would like to build there.

Then, draw yourself and your future spouse.

Next, draw a source of fresh drinking water.

Now, draw a source of food.

Is it rainy or sunny? Draw storm clouds or a bright sun.

Then, pick a number from one to five, and draw that many birds.

Finally, draw the same number of starfish.

Once you've finished, read on.

The house represents the wedding you want to have (not necessarily the wedding you're currently planning). The water source is the parents of the bride, and the food source is the parents of the groom. Clouds indicate that there's trouble brewing around your wedding; maybe one set of parents is divorced and causing problems. A sunny sky means that things are going smoothly, and even if there is a divorce in the family, it's not a real issue. The birds are the best man and groomsmen, and the starfish are the maid of honor and bridesmaids.

Now look at the relationships among the things you've drawn. Is your wedding a stately mansion, a humble cottage, or a rudimentary lean-to? How close are you standing to your future husband or wife? Are the parents providing abundant sustenance or just a little trickle? Is one of your birds or starfish looming larger than the rest, or are they all insignificant in the larger picture of your wedding? Compare your drawing with that of your fiancé and have a good laugh. Then, use the pictures as a starting point to seriously discuss the differences in your wedding expectations and your feelings about the wedding party.

Big Issues

····································

· Hers ·

BEING ENGAGED

ONCE you become engaged, you're a woman on a mission. Sure, you have a wedding to plan. But first, you have to inform the world that your status has changed from girlfriend to fiancée. For many of us, this realization sets in while the tears from the proposal are still wet on our cheeks. We're helping our husband-to-be get up off his knees, we look deeply into his eyes, and we say, "Where's the phone?" Our mothers, meanwhile, have been waiting years for that late-night call. Dave and I dated for a long time before we became engaged, and so the night he finally proposed and I called my mother at 11:30 P.M. to break the news, she was way ahead of me. All I said was, "Hi, Mom," and she replied, "Let's have the wedding next fall!"

There's a kind of honeymoon period before your actual honeymoon. It starts right after you say yes and ends with your first fight over passed versus buffet-style hors d'oeuvres. During this phase—usually about a week in duration—you'll find yourself coming up with creative new ways of getting people to notice your ring. For some reason, once the initial round of informative telephone calls is over, new fiancées turn coy and shy. We don't want to blurt it out—"Hey, I got engaged last night!"—we want to waltz into the office the next morning and have people fawn over us. We don't want to brag, we want people to *notice*. We feel different, after all, now that we're almost responsible married ladies, so surely we look different, too.

While you might, in fact, develop an engaged-woman glow, the sparkling ring on your finger is truly your most reliable advertisement. Short of taping the thing to your forehead, here are some tried-and-true techniques for putting your ring in people's sightline.

- The hairflip and behind-the-ear tuck

- Checking your manicure

- Pointing with your ringfinger instead of your forefinger

- Cracking only the knuckles of your right hand

- Taking up smoking—with your left hand

- Looking pensive—chin resting on left hand, left index finger resting thoughtfully on pursed lips

Despite your best efforts, your gestures may still go unrecognized. You must then say, "Notice anything different?" Sometimes the person you're speaking with is obtuse and will run through a laundry list of things like, "Uh...new haircut? Changed your nail polish color? Plucked your eyebrows? Bleached your moustache?" Eventually, he or she will get the point, and then you're free to launch into your telling of the Engagement Story.

Even if your fiancé proposed in the most doltish way imaginable, you must prepare yourself for Newly Engaged Week by building him into a master of technique. Did he propose while watching TV? You don't have to say it happened exactly like that. You can, instead, say that he rented your favorite romantic movie, froze the frame right where the hero proposes to his love, and knelt down right there on the TV room rug. If he proposed over the phone, you can tell people he called from the Concorde, returning from a business trip, on the anniversary of the exact time and day you first met. Remember, this is the fun part. You're about to enter planning hell, so milk the excitement of engagement while you can.

FREQUENTLY ASKED QUESTIONS DURING YOUR ENGAGEMENT PERIOD

Now that you've accepted a marriage proposal, you've entered a world where you eat, sleep, and breathe wedding plans. During this time, parents, friends, co-workers, and complete strangers will ask you the same four questions over and over and over again. Here they are, complete with sarcastic answers—since a courteous reply takes too much energy.

QUESTION: *So when's the wedding?*
POSSIBLE ANSWERS: a) This is it. Are you having fun?   b) We'll set the date the minute you get off my damn back!   c) I don't believe in the concept of time.

QUESTION: *Have you bought your dress yet?*
POSSIBLE ANSWERS: a) I'm making it myself out of Kleenex.   b) I wanted to get your opinion first. Whaddya think, leather or suede?   c) It's a nudist wedding.

QUESTION: *How did he propose?*
POSSIBLE ANSWERS: a) He said, "You wanna?" I said, "Yeah."   b) He got down on one knee, then I missed the rest when I ran to call my mother.   c) How did who propose?

QUESTION: *How do you like your future in-laws?*
POSSIBLE ANSWERS: a) Slightly poached.   b) 500 miles away.   c) How do you like the taste of sour milk?

· *His* ·

BEING ENGAGED

THERE are two times in a man's romantic life when he really shines. One is on his wedding day, and the other is the moment he proposes. Assuming you've already popped the question, if you did it right, you probably now have a great story to tell your friends, your children, and all the folks at work.

There's no doubt about it, telling the tale of your proposal is a competition. You're up against the most tear-jerking engagement stories in the history of mankind. The actor who, on the closing night of his play, knelt down and proposed to his girlfriend in the audience. The guy who took his true love to their favorite restaurant and arranged for the waiters to bring a surprise with every course—an "I Love You" card with the appetizer, a travel brochure of Greece with the salad, two plane tickets to Athens with the entree, and a diamond ring with dessert. And the classic Pepsi commercial where the cowboy arranges for an airplane skywriter to spell out "Marry me Sue." When Sue starts bawling and nods "Yes!" there isn't a dry eye at the hoedown. That's the reaction you're looking for when the women you work with ask you how you proposed. At the very least, you want an "Aaaawwww. That's so sweet!"

Engagement stories guaranteed to get this reaction have common elements: for example, proposing somewhere relevant (the place you first met, first kissed, or first watched *Say Anything* together); mentioning that you cried too (it's amazing, just saying those words at the end of an engagement story will make other women cry); kneeling (no matter where you were, no matter what the circumstances, if you didn't kneel, your story's no good); showing off a memento of the occasion as you tell the story (a flower that you kept, a wine bottle from the restaurant, a picture taken by a waiter).

When I proposed to Wendy I was kneeling on a dock near the field where we first kissed seven years earlier. I wasn't crying because we were both distracted by a stray cat in the field who meowed at us loudly, constantly, during the entire proposal. We later found the cat, and since he didn't have a collar and seemed desperate for a home, we gave him one. Our Engagement Kitty is a constant, furry reminder of a very special night in our lives, and I have a story that's particularly effective at eliciting "Aaaawwwws" from friends, colleagues, and total strangers.

Keep in mind, the engagement period is about more than great stories. It's a time to make sure you're doing the right thing, and to discuss issues you've never talked about before, such as what makes you happy, what you think you will and won't change about yourself, and what kind of life you want to be living in twenty years. Now's the time to agree on important marital issues, like whether you want children and how many, the extent to which religion is a part of your family, and how much money you'll need in order to be comfortable. Most people use the engagement period to plan a spectacular wedding, but it's essential that you make time during the next year to plan a lasting marriage as well.

· *Hers* ·

PREMARITAL EDUCATION

THE wedding planning process is a roiling cauldron of pressure that can create tension within even the strongest couples. But during the months before a wedding, warning signs may surface that indicate there's more than mere stress coming between the bride- and groom-to-be. It's not always easy to distinguish the difference between superficial and deep-seated problems, but a widespread failure to investigate the roots of any disagreements early on may be a factor contributing to this country's 50 percent divorce rate.

Premarital counseling is dramatically effective at providing couples with the skills necessary to weather tough spots in their relationships—both during the engagement period and in the years to come. But couples are often reluctant to seek the advice of a counselor or clergymember, even after they run into difficulties. It could be that seeking counseling feels too much like admitting the existence of a serious problem. Or there may be some truth to the perception that men are less comfortable seeking help than women are. A bride who suggests counseling could find that the suggestion alone creates more friction between her and her fiancé.

Many Catholic churches stipulate that engaged couples go through a series of counseling sessions with the officiating priest before he will perform the ceremony. Some states, like Florida, offer the option of a "contract marriage," in which couples go through premarital counseling and sign an agreement that makes it more difficult for them to later get a divorce. It's possible to look upon these things as intrusions into your private relationship, but on the other hand, it's hard to imagine how the guidance of a supportive third party could be anything other than beneficial.

Have you experienced any of the following during your engagement?

1. You've just had your eighth fight of the day about the same issue.

2. You're having wild dreams that always end the same way: you're standing at the altar with your fiancé answering "No" to the question, "Do you take this woman?"

3. You'd like to talk about issues like white or black tie for the groomsmen or how you feel about buying your first home, but you're afraid your fiancé will call off the wedding.

4. When you're confiding in a friend about the latest wedding snafu, she fills in the rest of your sentence by rote, "I know, I know. He just doesn't understand you, right?"

These disagreements, misunderstandings, and fears may all be the sort that will blow over once you and your new husband are safely honeymooning on a sunny beach sipping Bahama Mamas, but they could be symptomatic of deeper issues in your relationship. While your fiancé may rebel against the idea that there's anything going on other than a fight over spicy tuna rolls versus roasted pepper ravioli, disagreements bear investigating just to be on the safe side.

So rather than fighting it, why not make just one appointment for you and your fiancé with a counselor or therapist or rabbi or priest. Or try attending a weekend group meeting such as Engaged Encounter (visit the Web site www.wwme.org or call (909) 863-9963 for more information). Afterward, you may feel inclined to schedule regular counseling sessions for you alone or as a couple. At the very least, you'll gain more confidence in the short-term nature of your relationship difficulties and the long-term prospects for your love.

·*His*·

PREMARITAL EDUCATION

THE typical man's mantra is "If it ain't broke, don't fix it." You and your fiancée are getting married, right? So what is there to talk about besides planning the wedding? What is there to think about besides getting through this process so your lives can be normal again?

Well, for one thing, once you get the wedding over with, you'll be married, and if you think that life as husband and wife is pretty much the same as living together, you're headed for a surprise. Marriage is commitment with a capital C, and since you might not have been able to even say that word until recently, you may be woefully unprepared for its effect on your lifestyle.

Thanks to the stress of planning your wedding and the conflicting personalities of your families, you're probably going through relationship difficulties right now that you're too distracted to recognize. These may be minor problems of the sort married couples encounter every day, such as "You hurt my feelings," or "Why does my mother bother you so much?" Or they could be indicators of a basic difference in beliefs or a major underlying doubt, such as "If you say that one more time, so help me God, I'll call this whole thing off!"

Under the best of circumstances, it's difficult to convince most men that they need help, which is why we'll stand in one aisle of Home Depot for five hours trying to figure out the difference between two kinds of glue gun instead of asking the nearest employee to explain it to us. Premarital counseling is help of the most necessary kind, and whether it's required by your religious institution, suggested by your state government, or completely voluntary, you'll find that even one session with a professional counselor will do wonders for your relationship.

No doubt, you have excuses. And for those I have answers:

"Our relationship is different. We've never fought a day in our lives." I hate to burst your bubble, but someday, you *will* fight. What counseling can do is help you set aside the romantic vision of the relationship you've created — just for an hour or so — and look realistically at the challenges you'll face together. You can also learn techniques for making it through the fights you think you'll never have.

"I just want to get through this. Maybe we'll see someone after we're married." This sort of defeats the purpose. One of the rare but necessary results of premarital counseling is that certain highly incompatible couples realize they shouldn't get married until they grow a little more as individuals. If you find this out after you're married, you'll either end up incredibly unhappy or as another sad divorce statistic.

"My fiancée and I talk through our problems really well. What do I need someone else's opinion for?" If you're such a well-grounded couple, what are you afraid of? Talking with a professional, or in a group with other couples, might open your eyes to issues you never thought of. At the very least, it will help you gauge just how compatible you are. It's better than a *Cosmo* quiz.

"I don't want some stranger telling me I shouldn't marry the woman I love." Why would someone tell you that? The job of a priest or a counselor is to help you and your fiancée *strengthen* your marriage, and to give you the tools you need to solve problems more easily. If it scares you to ask yourself, "Am I

ready for marriage?" or if you're afraid your fiancée is having second thoughts, a counselor can help you face those concerns and answer them honestly. These professionals *want* you to get married, so they'll do everything they can to help you do it successfully.

When the excuses run out, and you allow yourself to be dragged into counseling, you may even enjoy it. Talking about yourself is kind of fun, especially when someone is telling you what a great couple you and your fiancée make, as your counselor is sure to do. Before you know it, you're on your way to weekly premarital counseling sessions, making friends with other couples there, and feeling like you're ready for all the headaches, late-night discussions, and baby vomit that marriage may bring. That and, of course, a lifetime of fulfillment and joy.

·*Hers*·

RELIGION AND CULTURE

WHEN Ethan, who is Protestant, married Jill, who is Jewish, Jill's parents insisted that Ethan convert to Judaism and that the ceremony be traditionally Jewish. They threatened to withhold any financial support unless they got their way. This, of course, spawned a debate over the religious tradition in which Ethan and Jill's children would be raised. Ethan wasn't particularly opposed to converting, but he didn't appreciate being forced into a major decision regarding children who weren't even born yet, and Jill wholeheartedly agreed. They told her parents, "We don't want your money. We'll send you an invitation to *our* wedding."

When Jill's mother started speaking to them again, they entered a delicate negotiation over the specific points of the dual-religion ceremony Ethan and Jill planned to have. They argued over whether a receiving line is Christian, over whether traditional Jewish customs like breaking the glass or having a huppah would be offensive to non-Jews. Unfortunately, after all the discussions, their officiant forgot to invite Jill's parents up to participate in the vows—a point that had been negotiated and agreed upon in advance—and

Jill's mother whispered to him, "Thanks for ruining my only daughter's wedding."

While some couples battle their parents over issues of religion, others find their biggest challenge is overcoming cultural differences. Some of the most complicated and frustrating wedding scenarios involve both.

Ada's family was from New York City, and her mother was Catholic. Her fiancée, Barry, was from North Carolina and his family was Southern Baptist. When they began planning their wedding, they quickly discovered that their differences went well beyond matters of faith. The wedding was to be held in the South, where receptions typically involve cake and punch and peanuts served in the basement of the church where the ceremony was held. Ada and her family, on the other hand, expected a traditional Northern wedding with a formal meal served in a formal setting.

The religion question was quickly settled; Ada herself is not that religious so the ceremony was held in a Southern Baptist church. But in planning the reception, she ran into serious culture clash. A true New Yorker, Ada insisted on getting things in writing, but the contractors in North Carolina were long accustomed to verbal agreements. She wanted to taste the food of prospective caterers, who had never heard of such a thing: "What, give you samples of food for free before the wedding? Everyone knows our food is wonderful!"

When asked to suggest lodgings for out-of-town guests and for the wedding couple, Ada's local wedding planner recommended the nearby Best Western, which had a honeymoon suite. It was probably a perfectly nice hotel, but one that Ada felt was absolutely unsuitable for the expectations of her New York City friends and relatives. Because of the culture gap, her planner had no way of anticipating Ada's tastes, so Ada ended up spelling out every detail of what she wanted, using pictures ripped from magazines. The cultural differences turned out to be more easily resolved than the religious differences, which had long-term repercussions. To this day, Ada's mother has not forgiven her for being married outside the Catholic church.

There are lessons to be drawn from the experiences of other couples. It's most important to build a bridge between religions and cultures that will satisfy both you and your fiancé, even if it doesn't necessarily make every family member happy. Your wedding doesn't have to be exclusively Catholic, Jewish, Hindu, or another faith. simply because your parents want it to be. But if you want them to be happy and you truly respect their beliefs, consider incorporating the best traditions from your families' religions into a personalized ceremony. Many couples ask two officiants, one from each faith, to perform their wedding, and some go as far as holding two different religious ceremonies on two different days.

Despite the stern demands of parents and the raised voices of engaged couples everywhere, the mixture of religion and weddings can create some funny situations. One bride thought she knew exactly what she was going to get when she called 1-800 Dial-a-Priest. She was assigned Minister Michael, who did an admirable job officiating her wedding. At the reception, a guest pulled the bride and groom aside and said, "Now I recognize the man who married you. That's Rabbi Michael from the Silverstein wedding!"

His

RELIGION AND CULTURE

THERE are some people, perhaps some very close to you (okay, your parents) who may believe that they should dictate the religious aspects of your wedding. Their family belief structure has been passed down through the ages since God was trying to plan his (or her) own wedding, and by all that is holy, you *will* keep their faith. This isn't a problem as long as you were raised with these beliefs, you still hold them sacred, and your fiancée feels the same way. Otherwise, as it has so many times throughout history, religion is about to start a war.

No doubt, there are a million things you would rather do to prepare for your wedding than fight with your parents over issues of faith. Suddenly, registering for flatware seems pretty intriguing. And hey, let's plow through that fifty-pound book of nearly identical invitations! But unpleasant as it may seem, you absolutely *must* talk to your parents, and to your fiancée's parents, about their religious expectations. The reason is logistical: the inclusion of religion can affect everything at a wedding from who performs the ceremony to where the families sit, from where the ceremony is held to what you'll eat at the reception, from how the receiving line is ordered to what you do with the bridal bouquet. You need to know what your parents expect early on, so you can either bring it in line with what you want, or give in to what they want without reversing plans that have already been made. Nine times out of ten, this discussion will be reasonable, pleasant, and over in fifteen minutes.

Then there are the unlucky couples. If you're just slightly unlucky, the conversation with your parents will be a simple matter of winnowing out what is absolutely crucial to them. For instance, "All we really want, dear, is for you to get a personal blessing from the Pope." *Horribly* unlucky couples—usually those who come from very orthodox religious families and are about to enter interfaith marriages—receive an unconditional mandate from above. "You will be married by our rabbi and only our rabbi, every man will wear a yarmulke, the ceremony will be three hours long and entirely in Hebrew, you will serve only Manishewitz, and Elijah will receive an invitation."

Perhaps unlucky is too kind a term for this situation. A better word is unfair. You and your fiancée are about to embark on a new life together. You'll be expected to rely on your own intelligence, education, and force of will to succeed in a world that is, day by day, growing more populous and more complicated. And as a bon voyage present, your parents deliver unto you a "Do it our way or else" ultimatum?

No, no, and no again. Today you're freer than ever before to choose the aspects of religion and culture that should be incorporated into your wedding. This is an important freedom, especially with the proliferation of interfaith marriages over the last few decades. It's totally up to you and your fiancée to decide whether you want a traditional wedding in one religion, a harmonious mixture of two, an amalgam of all your favorite traditions, or a simple, legally binding affair with no religious influence.

This is your wedding, and it's time you got your way. Tell your parents what you want. Tell them you would be happy to accommodate them as long as their wishes don't interfere with your and your future wife's plans. And, if nothing else works, tell them that you won't need their money and that they'll receive an invitation a month or two before the wedding.

This sounds tough. To some, such a face-off even sounds impossible. But if you put the needs of your parents above those of your fiancée, you'll only dread your wedding more with every approaching day. It's far better to put your foot down and get what you want early, so your parents have time to cool off and realize how silly they're being. And it's best to let time and the magnetic bonds of familial love smooth out these differences, even if the resentment doesn't lift until after the wedding. Difficult as it is to imagine now, these major blowouts almost always turn into blurry memories once they're in your rear-view mirror.

ORIGINS OF POPULAR WEDDING TRADITIONS

The exchange of metal rings—conceived independently by Hebrew, Parsi, classical Roman, and Christian cultures.

The bridal veil—originally orange in ancient Rome, and white in Christian and Slavic societies.

A crown of flowers—again from the Romans, originally composed of marjoram and verbena, and later, of myrtle and orange blossoms.

A marriage pavilion or canopy—from the ancient Etruscans of Italy. Hebrews used a closed tent, and later a silk or tapestry canopy to symbolize the nuptial chamber. Hindus and Parsis separated the bride and the groom by a curtain within a pavilion.

The bouquet—long considered a symbol of happiness, the bouquet was originally part of a binding floral motif worn by both the bride and the groom.

The garter—started in France, where elements of the bride's clothing were symbols of luck.

· Hers ·

COLD FEET AND STAGE FRIGHT

THE nice thing about being a bride rather than a groom is that you can become preoccupied by so many wedding details that you're completely distracted from thinking about how your life is going to change once you're married. Who's pondering the seriousness of a lifetime commitment when there are so many things to do, do, do? Even if you start to get a funny feeling in the pit of your stomach, like "Oh, my god, I'm about to..." when you're sitting down to review your vows, it's awfully easy to squash that little voice and find something else that needs taking care of.

Don't kid yourself. What you're about to do is huge, and even if you pretend you're not thinking about it, your subconscious will do it for you. Many brides report having recurring prewedding dreams in which they find themselves tending a flock of sheep in lace veils, or walking down the aisle naked, or being dragged to the bottom of a lake by the weight of their wedding gown. One bride was cool as a cucumber throughout the planning process, and while getting dressed and made up on the big day, but found herself frozen in place as the processional music begin.

No matter how certain you are about your choice of groom, no matter how level-headed you are about the planning of your wedding, there's no getting around the fact that getting married involves strong emotions that must be dealt with somehow, some way. For many brides, these emotions come out in a particular aspect of the planning process that just won't go right. Dave and I had been together for so long before we got married that I never consciously gave a second thought to the significance of what we were about to do—until I wondered, in retrospect, why I had been absolutely incapable of committing to a wedding dress. It's easier to let out natural feelings through being weepy and overwrought while trying to resolve difficult wedding issues than it is to admit to yourself that you're about to make a huge life change, and that's the real reason you're feeling this way.

> ## SEVEN SURVIVAL TIPS FOR CALMING WEDDING-DAY JITTERS
>
> 1. Imagine the officiant in his underwear—or better yet, wearing yours.
> 2. Take a look at your mother. Now *that's* nervous!
> 3. Take three deep, cleansing breaths. Of nitrous oxide.
> 4. Pray to the God of Wedding Bands That Don't Stink.
> 5. Eat something, anything, preferably with a side of Valium.
> 6. Imagine yourself on your honeymoon, lying on the beach. Your mother's screaming is nothing but the calls of seagulls.
> 7. On the organ: "Here Comes the Bride." In your head: "Saturday Night Fever."

We've been conditioned to believe that on her wedding day, a bride should be filled with pure joy and light and happiness and excitement—no sadness at saying goodbye to the previous phase of her life; no bittersweet feeling of apprehension that the road ahead may have potholes. A bride-to-be tends not to articulate her fear of sneezing during the ceremony and having nowhere to turn for a Kleenex, or ruining the makeup job of her life with tears of joy.

But all your married friends have been there, and all of them can attest to the fact that, when you're standing with your fiancé in front of a minister or rabbi or justice of the peace, you may be hit by extremely powerful feelings. It's important to prepare for that moment by talking to other people about the experience of getting and being married. You won't be able to prevent the emotions from pouring out—who wants to anyway?—but you can get a solid understanding of what to expect, so you don't end up so overwhelmed that you forget what happened at your own wedding.

· *His* ·

COLD FEET AND STAGE FRIGHT

WHY in the world would anyone be nervous about his own wedding? Perhaps because you'll be professing your deepest love in front of every friend and relative you have. Or maybe because you'll be responding to the question "Do you promise to love and to cherish this woman for as long as you both shall live?" with the words "I do." And let's not forget the fact that backing out now—or worse, at the altar like Hugh Grant did in *Four Weddings and a Funeral*—would send four parents and one ex-fiancée ballistic and make you feel like the biggest jerk in the universe.

So there are a few good reasons to dread the most important day of your life, but none you can't deal with if you prepare properly. To help, here are the five best pieces of advice we've gathered from couples who've walked down that fearsome aisle and made it back alive as husband and wife:

1. Why worry when nobody's looking at you? Think about what's expected of the groom at most weddings. He should be gracious, cheerful, quiet, and do what he's told. Man, anybody can do that! Because your fiancée has been dreaming of this day ever since she was a little girl, because primarily her parents are responsible for hosting a successful wedding, and because people don't waste their breath singing "Here Comes the Groom" or whispering "My, what a lovely tuxedo he's wearing," you can safely assume that most of the pressure is going to fall on the bride. Put your energy into comforting and reassuring her, and there won't be much left over to waste on your own nerves.

2. *Make sure there's enough time to do everything you want to do.* Some powerhouse couples like to plan the ultimate weekend getaway for their bridal party to thank them for being in their wedding. The itineraries could put Caribbean cruise lines to shame:

8:00 A.M., breakfast

9:00 A.M., brisk five-mile run

10:00 A.M., shuffleboard

10:30 A.M., bobbing for apples

11:00 A.M., get fitted for tuxedos

11:30 A.M., run for Congress

12:00 P.M., lunch

Planning a fun weekend around your wedding is a great idea, but keep in mind that you have to execute everything you plan. It's hard enough coordinating a wedding without having to make sure everyone shows up for the Sunday morning hayride. And remember, people need time to read the paper, take a nap, and go to the bathroom once in a while. Your guests will be more appreciative of the extracurricular activities you plan for them if you also provide a bit of time to breathe. In the end, that means more relaxed guests and fewer worries for you.

3. *Work out before the ceremony.* A shot of scotch in the back room with your best man may be the traditional way to soothe the groom's nerves before

a wedding, but a far more effective method is a quick game of tennis. Or a run on the treadmill, a bike ride around town, or a few laps in the hotel pool. Working out before taking the big plunge not only allows you to use up some excess energy, it gives you a chance to think about what a great day this is going to be for you.

4. *If something goes wrong, great! You can laugh about it later.* There are only two people who will remember every little screwup at your wedding: you and your wife. The rest of your guests probably won't notice, and if they do, it'll make for great stories you can all laugh about at the next wedding. Nobody is coming to your wedding to find fault with you, and nobody expects everything to be perfect. As long as you say the right names in the vow—"I (blank) take you (blank) to be my lawful wedded wife"—no one is going to sue you for incompetent matrimonial process.

5. *Your wedding isn't about getting it right. It's about love.* No matter what your vows say, no matter how you say them, no matter how many people are in the audience, no matter how long it took to finally get to this point, the only thing that you absolutely, positively have to be sure of when you make this commitment is that you love the woman you're about to marry. You can't do this for her sake, or for her parents'. Marriage is as selfish as it is selfless, in that you should be doing it to ensure your own personal happiness as well as your wife's. Doubts about when, where, and how to get married are all perfectly acceptable, but "whether" should never be in question. Let your absolute faith in your love for your fiancée carry you through the day's events. If you need courage and reassurance, you'll find it in her eyes.

· Hers ·

HITTING THE WALL

THERE you are, mowing down your wedding To Do list like a twenty-five-horsepower Toro tractor through a field of sock-high bluegrass. The dress is ordered, the deposits are made, the invitations are addressed, and you've even remembered to buy a gross of votive candles to illuminate every nook and cranny of the fabulous old mansion where a violin trio will serenade the two hundred guests celebrating your nuptials over a gourmet meal. There's only one problem: the mansion's owners have just informed you that there can be no open flames on the grounds—not even a teensy candle or two.

Why is everyone conspiring against you? You're not asking for the moon, after all. You just want things to be perfect.

You whine, you cajole, you plead, you cry. You understand the owners have had problems in the past with a couple of curtains catching on fire, but you'd be *soooo* careful, and, after all, that was some other bozo's highly inferior wedding. Can't an exception be made for you?

No dice. You will have no shimmering candlelight. But you can congratulate yourself on hitting your first wall. It's almost a foregone conclusion that at some point before you say "I do," someone along the way will tell you, "I won't." The caterer won't substitute rice for pasta for your nieces who are allergic to flour. The florist can't find a way to get peonies in November. You're in the one-week countdown, and those ten pounds are not coming off. You've done the math over and over, but there's no way you can afford prime rib *and* chicken.

This is the point in every wedding when what you want runs smack up against what you can have, and what you want invariably loses. Sometimes you hit other people's limits, and sometimes you hit a limit that is self-imposed. You reach a point where you simply can't handle one more special request, one more unique need, one more problem to solve. You're out of time, out of money, out of patience. You've had it up to here, and you can't imagine why you didn't just take your parents up on their offer to give you a lump sum of cash in lieu of a formal wedding.

When you run up against the wall of limitations, you have two options. One, you can turn the matter over to your fiancé. Sometimes a different head can look at the same problem but see a new way to solve it. Bringing your fiancé in will make you feel as though you're not alone in the world with the roadblock, whatever it is.

Your second course of action in dealing with limitations is to turn belly up. That's right, surrender. It's difficult to picture it now, but in a few months you'll barely be able to remember that your bridesmaids refused to dye their hair the same color; so in the thick of wedding-planning nightmares, you must sometimes take a deep breath, give in, and move on.

Never in human history has there been a perfect wedding, and you can give yourself a bleeding ulcer if you're unable to accept that yours won't be the first. Sometimes people are selfish jerks. Sometimes brides are overwrought. You may not be in a mental position to clearly see the difference, so take a deep breath and ask yourself if you can possibly go on without getting what you want.

His

HITTING THE WALL

EVEN if you're planning a wedding in an open field, you will, at some point in the process, run head-on into a wall. Maybe that wall will come in the form of the manager of a reception hall telling you that what you want is exactly what you can't have. Possibly it's a completely unreasonable ultimatum laid down by your parents or by your fiancée's parents. Your wall could be budgetary, religious, geographical, meteorological, congressional, or karmic, but no matter where it comes from, it will surely seem unscalable.

All your life, you've been learning how to solve big problems by yourself. Now, perhaps for the first time, you're faced with a problem that you have to solve with another person, your fiancée, as a team. This is no time to panic. The two of you can climb even the highest wall together once you learn the right skills.

Let's take an example from real life. James and Gail wanted their reception to be a real party, with a mix of music everyone could dance to, including five specific songs that were important to them. Gail's parents insisted that they get a band, so they set out to find one that could play what they wanted. Of the two bands they liked, one refused to play anything but its own established set list, and the other was willing to learn only two of the five specific song requests.

James suggested that a DJ would be able to play all the songs they wanted, plus the original versions of all the traditional wedding songs those bands were going to play anyway, at a fraction of a band's cost. So, he proposed, maybe Gail's parents would change their minds about the band when they saw how happy a DJ would make their daughter. But Gail's parents' answer was swift and decisive. No friends of theirs would be caught dead at a wedding with a *discotheque jockey*.

And so James and Gail arrived at the wall, imposed upon them by one set of stubborn parents and a horde of wedding bands that willingly played ballrooms, but just wouldn't play ball. This couple got over their hurdle by using the following proven problem-solving skills.

1. *They didn't blame each other.* Instead they treated the problem itself as the enemy in this case and joined together to beat it.

2. *They stayed focused on the current issue.* Statements like "Your parents are always forcing things down our throats," or "Why can't you ever stand up to my father," were banned from James and Gail's conversation. While both of these observations may have pointed to deeper problems, they weren't helpful in solving *this* problem.

3. *They stayed positive and kept brainstorming.* "We're screwed" may be the first thing that comes to most couples' minds, but these two made sure they started their sentences with, "What if we tried..."

4. *They kept everyone's needs on the bargaining table.* Before sacrificing their own wishes (the five crucial songs) or Gail's parents' wishes (the band) or the wishes of the most likely band (two new songs, no more), they tried to imagine scenarios in which everyone's needs could exist in the same place and time.

Here's what James and Gail came up with. In one brainstorming session, they realized that the band had to take breaks throughout the evening. They decided to ask the band if, during their breaks, they would play CDs of the songs they refused to learn. The band agreed. Gail's parents said fine. They got their band; the band got their gig; James and Gail got their songs. And everybody got over the wall.

Cool heads and quick minds may be invaluable assets when you hit limits like this one during your wedding planning. But there's just no substitute for positive problem-solving skills both before and after your wedding day.

· *Hers* ·

LOSING PERSPECTIVE

HYPERORGANIZED, full of energy, and determined to have a better wedding than all their friends, many brides-to-be take to wedding planning like ducks to water. No detail shall be left to chance; no problem unresolved; no voice of dissent unsquashed. One bride insisted the baker dye the icing on her cake to exactly match her off-white dress. Another woman was reduced to tears when she couldn't find the right width silver cord with which to tie the birdseed sachets—gold was available, but she had a silver theme going with the ink on the invitations, programs, and thank-you notes, the platinum-colored bridesmaids' dresses, the bridesmaids' jewelry, the napkin rings, and the ribbons in the floral arrangements.

For such brides, the toughest part of the planning process is not when they have five thousand things to take care of, but when all five thousand things are done and there's nothing left to worry about. That's when they start going over and over every aspect of the wedding, looking for imperfections and inferior choices to correct while there's still time.

When I talk to brides a few months or a few years after their weddings, their biggest regret is invariably that they didn't calm down and take the whole thing less seriously *at the time*. The last thing you want is to feel in retrospect like you've blown an entire year of your life for four hours of showmanship. With six months left to go, Natalie told me: "My wedding feels like a big display of how organized I am. Everyone is going to be judging how I pull this off." She's been losing sleep because she has exactly six and a half minutes of music to accompany the seven groupings of bridal party members walking down the aisle, and hasn't yet figured out how to make sure everyone starts walking at precise forty-five-second intervals.

Natalie is hardly unusual. Frankly, the exception to the rule is the bride who is able to keep her wedding in perspective while in the middle of planning it. It's terrifyingly easy to get so wound up in creating the event of the century that you forget a wedding is really meant to be just a big party.

The truth is, no one else is thinking about your wedding nearly as much as you are—either now or at the event itself. All guests want is to have a good time, eat, drink, dance a little, cough up a gift, wish you well, and then go home and rest up before the next wedding. People will always find things to criticize, but there's absolutely nothing you can do to forestall it. You can't predict every single thing that could potentially be complained about, and you couldn't solve every problem even if you knew about it. The same understated floral arrangements that your boss found "refreshingly lovely" will probably come across as cheap and chintzy to your grandmother.

Barbra Streisand, who recently got married at age fifty-six, collected ideas and photos for about a year. Then she planned the event like a major theatrical production. The decorative flowers matched the rugs, which matched the flower girls' baskets, head wreaths, and dresses. The flowers on the tables echoed the colors of the china service. Barbra even recorded an album inspired by the planning period. Yes, my friends, this is a shining example of Lost Perspective. In contrast, Cindy Crawford got married on the beach. She let her guests sit wherever they wanted. There was a small dance floor and at the end of the evening everyone ended up in the pool. Which of these two weddings would you rather have attended?

Trust me, you will feel differently about your wedding when it's over than you did when you were planning it. I was very happy with my wedding, but I remember turning up my nose when a relative offered the use of her beautiful backyard for the reception. Looking back on it now, that backyard reception seems like it would have been fun, and a lot less expensive than the formal reception we ended up having. Several new brides have said their parents offered them a choice between a lump sum of cash or a lavish wedding. At the time, they couldn't imagine taking the money and eloping, forgoing the blowout wedding. Afterward, however, eloping seemed much more viable.

Remember, life is long, and a wedding takes only a few months out of it. After the reception, you'll still need those same friends whom you're currently alienating because you can't manage to talk about anything but peu de soie. Midway through planning her wedding, my friend Laura suddenly realized, "I could turn into a prima donna right now, but if I do no one will like me afterward." What she—like all brides—learned from experience is this: it's not the perfect wedding that makes you feel married, it's getting married itself. And that you can do anywhere, anytime, with or without a cake that matches your dress.

· His ·

LOSING PERSPECTIVE

LOSING perspective while planning your wedding is a phenomenon tolerable only in the following people:

- Movie stars going for marriage number three (or higher)

- People with huge bags of money and nothing productive to do

- Those planning a "royal" wedding

- Those who are nuts

If none of these descriptions fit you, there's no excuse for letting your wedding take on a monstrous life all its own. The bride who required all her guests to arrive in full Elizabethan period costumes surely could have found more constructive ways to use her energy. And somebody should have had a long talk with the groom who insisted that each of his ushers repeat, in the style of *The Dirty Dozen*, a rhyming mnemonic about the order of events in the ceremony—"One, the bride hits the aisle; Two, we all stop and smile; Three, the groom says 'I do'; Four, the minister is through."

As these two examples illustrate, when it comes to weddings, men and women go overboard in completely different ways. A groom's overreactions tend to fall into the category of double-, triple-, and quadruple-checking plans to make sure everything runs smoothly, while a bride usually focuses her energy on making everything match down to the smallest detail.

As a result of these differences between the sexes, you'll need to take these two tests: one to see if you're losing perspective, and one to see if your fiancée is. In order to recognize when things are getting out of control, you should be able to detect the warning signs. Ask yourself the following questions:

1. Have you called the limousine service pretending you forgot what time the driver was supposed to arrive, just to make sure he has it right?

2. Have you done that more than once?

3. Did you put the checks for the minister, caterer, bartender, and photographer in separate, color-coded envelopes *and* separate pockets of your tux so they won't... mingle?

4. Have you drawn a diagram of where each liquor bottle should go behind the bar, taking care to separate clears from browns?

5. Do you have your tuxedo coat and pants, cuff links and studs, dress shirt, nice belt, dress shoes, dress socks, and underwear all on the same hanger?

6. Are you requiring the caterer to set each place at the tables with a water glass, champagne flute, red wine glass, white wine glass, juice glass, tumbler, coffee cup and saucer, and seven coasters?

7. Did you write a booklet for each usher and groomsman entitled "Where I should stand and what I should do every second of [your name here]'s wedding"?

If you answered yes to any of these questions, you'll be doing your heart (and your guests) a big favor if you go into the bathroom, take three deep breaths, and *chill out*! You will have a lot more fun at your wedding if you don't worry so much over the arrangements. If you allow yourself to trust that you organized everything correctly from the start, chances are your wedding will run smoothly. And if there are minor glitches, you'll probably be the only one who notices.

Now let's see how your fiancée is holding up. Do any of the following describe her behavior?

1. Has she suggested guest attire on the wedding invitation, complete with helpful color swatches?

2. Is the "Ice Sculptures" section of her Yellow Pages torn out?

3. On your reception program, under entertainment, does it say "Lords of the Dance"?

4. Have you caught her applying decorator paint to any of the following: flowers, ribbons, napkins, or her own hair?

5. Has she asked you how good you are at constructing theatrical sets?

6. Has she checked into the viability of saying your vows while seated atop an albino Bengal tiger?

7. Will her dress require "handlers"?

If you answered yes to any of these questions, it's time you and your fiancée had a little chat. There is a place for spectacle, but your guests are not buying tickets to your wedding, nor do they give a flying ferret what color the foie gras is. It may help to explain to your fiancée that her ambition is appreciated, and that you know she's working hard toward making your wedding more memorable. Tell her you'll remember your wedding fondly even if the fork handles clash with the food palette. And as long as your guests get a free meal at the end of the day, they'll be happy to see that the two of you are happy.

Crumple up those ice sculpture listings and go see a movie together. Your wedding plans can wait one more night.

· *Hers* ·

ROMANCE

IN a recent Gallup poll, 47 percent of the couples surveyed felt they spent too little time together. You may feel just the opposite in the months before your wedding, since you and your fiancé are seemingly spending every waking moment jointly interviewing caterers, auditioning bands, and looking at reception sites. The problem is, what you're experiencing is quantity, rather than quality time. This is basically a rehearsal for marriage itself, where the time situation doesn't get any better unless you take action to change it.

Starting now and continuing through the rest of your years together, you'll notice how easy it is to get caught up in the details of life while neglecting to appreciate it. It's important, therefore, to take the bull by the horns early, by injecting love and romance into the detail-orgy that makes up the planning of the average wedding.

We've all been to weddings in which the bride sweeps around officiously in her big white dress, barking out last-minute orders and barely stopping to say hello to her father before she starts criticizing the speed at which he's walking her down the aisle. At the altar waits the groom, who basically just did what he was told and showed up on time, bemused and more than a little frightened by the prospect of watching the top of his fiancée's head blow off should anything dare to go wrong. When these two get married, it's more like a business deal than a pledge of eternal love, and you can almost see the wheels spinning in the bride's mind as she marches across the room to whip the photographer into shape.

The way to avoid creating this scenario yourself is to build little oases of romance into your planning process. What could you add to every aspect of your wedding that would remind you and your fiancé of the point of it all? When you're planning the music, instruct the band or DJ to play "your" song at a key moment—the one that was playing in the background as you kissed for the first time. As you're picking the site for the reception, think: Is there a place that's meaningful to your relationship? If you met in college, perhaps there's a beautiful old mansion near your alma mater that hosts weddings.

Try to arrange little romantic gestures at the last minute. If your husband likes to eat pizza for breakfast, lunch, and dinner, why not surprise him by having the caterer prepare a special wedding meal of pizza for two? One couple made sure that they were staying in a different hotel from their guests. They wanted to make a grand exit at the end of the evening and preserve the romance of the event by disappearing.

I know it's tough to think romantically when you have so much to do. But in the midst of all the business-like details, it's important to try to remember the time when you and your fiancé first were a couple, before you got into that fight over the seating arrangements and the fifty-three other arguments over the food. Before you turned into the kind of people who cared just a little too much about small satin pillows and black bow ties.

· His ·

ROMANCE

FUNNY that you should need to be reminded about romance on what is supposed to be the most romantic day of your life. Yet, after months of planning and big-ticket transactions, the wedding ceremony can seem more like a business meeting than a celebration of love. It's sort of like the commercialization of Christmas, or celebrating birthdays as adults. We forget that these were once wondrous occasions filled with warm emotions and tender feelings, and we end up going through the motions wishing only for no screwups and the peace that will come when it's all over.

If you don't take some time to put a little romance back into your wedding day, or at least appreciate that which already exists, you may come to regret it later. Fortunately, romance isn't so hard to achieve once you set your mind to it. In fact, you can probably think of dozens of ways to make your fiancée feel she's the luckiest woman in the world. To get you started, here are a few that I've gathered from recent weddings.

Give gifts to each other. After all the money and time you've invested and all the gifts you're sure to receive from guests, it may seem redundant to purchase yet another token of your love. But imagine how happy your fiancée would be if you presented her with a pair of earrings that match her eyes. And how would you feel if she gave you the watch you've always wanted, inscribed on the back with your wedding date? Your gifts don't have to be expensive, just personal, meaningful tokens of affection given before the wedding to wish yourselves luck and happiness in your future together.

Inscribe your wedding rings. The plan is for this piece of metal to remain on your finger until death and beyond. Wouldn't it be nice if it contained a personal message from your true love? You could inscribe her ring after the wedding, but it will be a whole lot more powerful if you slip it onto her finger with your thoughts in place.

Add meaningful rituals to the ceremony. Gestures like using two candles to light one larger candle, reading passages or poems to each other at the altar, and holding a silk handkerchief between you as you say your vows are all beautiful ways to add romance to your wedding. Do a little research into wedding history and you're sure to find a romantic ritual that suits your style.

Do something special at your wedding. Hopefully you have some talent for performance that you're unafraid to share, such as playing an instrument, singing, or writing a poem. Any kind of personal tribute at your wedding will raise the romance quotient considerably. If you would prefer not to share your feelings in public, then prepare something special to say or play for your new wife on your wedding night. She's been crying all day, so why stop now?

Remind yourself to enjoy the moment. The best wedding advice one couple received was to take five minutes out of every hour during the reception, find a quiet spot together, and just take it all in. Every time they did it, they realized how special it was to have all their friends and family there with them, and how lucky they were to have found each other.

THE BIG ISSUE INK BLOT TEST

Let's do a little free association to see how you're feeling about the big issues in your wedding. Look at the following ink blots and pick the best description of what you see for each one. Then ask your soon-to-be husband or wife to do the same, and discuss any issues that come up.

a) an engagement ring
b) a man on his knees proposing
c) $20,000 in debt

a) a wedding cake
b) a bridal bouquet
c) cold, hard, stupefying terror

---

a) a lamb chop
b) a lobster tail
c) a stupid caterer who says you can't afford anything

a) a church

b) a synagogue

c) a bloody battle to the death with your parents

---

a) a beautiful flower

b) a lovely centerpiece

c) the flowers that ate Manhattan

a) a heart

b) true love

c) your wedding pictures after the photographer forgets to take the lens cap off

Arrangements

....

Hers
....

THE BUDGET

THERE are many aspects of the traditional Western wedding that a woman just doesn't want to think about too deeply, such as the fact that one or both of your parents is "giving you away," the idea of losing your birth name—and the expectation that your parents should pay for the wedding. Truth be told, the traditional budget arrangement in which your parents foot 95 percent of the bill is a holdover of the days when a bride was essentially chattel: currency handed off from the old patriarchy to a budding one.

It's no wonder that, in order to avoid both the symbolic and the logistical problems of the traditional budget arrangement, more and more couples are paying for their wedding themselves. After all, when you're footing the bill, your parents have a lot less leverage for getting their way. So you neatly avoid ultimatums like, "Serve duck for dinner and you'll have to go out and shoot them yourself, 'cause your ma and I aren't paying more than twenty-five dollars a plate."

The problem is, paying for your wedding can be like putting a down payment on a house. In New York City, where Dave and I live, weddings that cost $100,000 are common enough that caterers consider them midrange; the lower end is around $25,000. A $500 wedding dress is unheard-of—the most common range is $1,200–$2,000 and top-of-the-line gowns run $3,000–$10,000.

There are all kinds of books that offer concrete tips to help you plan a great wedding on a budget. Dave and I read many of them, and ended up feeling like the sixty dollars we spent on books would have been put to better use helping pay for shrimp instead of chicken in the pasta. The most important thing, we realized, is that whatever sum of money you possess is enough to host a perfectly satisfying wedding.

The trick is to set your priorities early and stick to them. Linda and her husband, Brad, decided that they would rather have a big party for all their friends than a fancy wedding at a fancy place with fancy food. So they held a nuptial picnic at a friend's beach house. After wracking their brains for months trying to figure out how to host a $25,000 wedding on a $6,000 budget, Amy and Mark decided upon a quiet, intimate wedding at a local restaurant with fifty guests. They figured there was no need to try to impress their guests with a wedding they couldn't afford, and, after all, dead broke is no way to start a marriage.

In fact many couples look back on their wedding and wish they had spent less money "impressing" their guests and more on making them comfortable and happy. After our wedding, Dave and I realized that we had budgeted a great deal of money for flowers and decorations, when we really should have invested in higher quality food. By going through your budget early and putting each item under the headings "Trying to Impress" and "Aiming to Please," you may be able to reallocate your resources to create a better party rather than a more spectacular show.

Unfortunately, some brides aren't even allowed to look at the finances. Sally's wedding, for instance, was entirely financed by her husband's parents, because her in-laws wanted a certain kind of event that her own parents couldn't afford. Her in-laws never gave Sally a budget and she always felt too uncomfortable to ask for one. She would show them options for catering and flowers, which they never felt were nice enough. After her mother-in-law arranged for the reception site, hired the florist she had used all her life, and commissioned a super-premium cake at fifteen dollars a slice, Sally finally resigned herself to the fact that her wedding was really her mother-in-law's affair.

Setting a wedding budget always involves stretching one dollar to cover two dollars' worth of goods, but when you're dealing with someone else's money, it adds an extra level of tension. Tempers will flare, and emotions will heat up, especially if either set of parents is divorced. Your parents may get frustrated if their finances don't mesh with your wishes and their dreams for you. As the instigator of this whole business, it's your job to be sensitive to your parents' feelings. Let them know that you'll be happy with whatever they can contribute. And remember, between you and your parents, money and love are entirely separate things. The lack of the former by no means implies the absence of the latter.

·*His*·

THE BUDGET

THE average wedding costs about sixteen thousand dollars. In determining your own budget relative to that number, much depends on the part of the country where you plan to get married (in New York City, the band alone may cost sixteen thousand dollars), the number of guests you plan to invite, and the size of your fiancée's parents' checkbook.

Before you can begin to look seriously for wedding services, such as the caterer, florist, and photographer, it's essential that you know where your wedding money is going to come from, and how much is coming. Since the majority of the wedding costs are traditionally covered by the bride's parents, the first thing you have to do is find out how much your future in-laws are willing to pay. We recommend you hold a preliminary budget meeting with them to make sure you're all in the same ballpark. It may feel uncomfortable at first, as if you're begging your fiancée's parents for money, but remember you're talking about their little girl and hopefully they, like you, want nothing but the best for her.

The problem comes when parents realize that "the best" costs ten times as much as it did when they got married. So if they haven't done any serious financial planning for this moment, you may have to look for alternate sources of funding. That's something you'll want to know early in the process, and a preliminary budget meeting is the perfect way to find out. Treat it like a business conference where you are the chairman and moderator. Your agenda could go something like this:

1. I'm marrying your daughter and that's fine with everyone, right?

2. You're going to pay for most of the wedding, right?

3. This is the kind of wedding we envision. Okay?

4. This is what we think it will cost. Does that sound reasonable?

5. Would you like to append or delete any items from this plan?

6. Since we're asking for so much, the least I can do is get the check for lunch. Thanks for coming.

In a best-case scenario, your fiancee's parents will stop you at point one and say, "All we want is for our daughter to be happy, and we're pleased to welcome you into the family. Whatever you two want to spend is fine with us." Then you can dispense with the formality and forge ahead with your plans, remembering to keep your in-laws apprised of costs and involve them in decisions whenever possible. In alternate scenarios, in-laws will give you a bottom-line number that they can afford, and you'll have to work around it. Or sometimes, in-laws will simply throw up their hands and say they wish they could help you, but if you want to marry their daughter, you're going to have to finance it yourselves.

A meeting like this is a controlled way to bring the topic of money out in the open. Any feelings of embarrassment or resentment can be discussed calmly, among adults. This is the time to bring up sticky issues, like the things you'd like to spend big money on, and find out how your future in-laws feel about these items. It's a good way to avoid nightmare scenes on the day of the ceremony, such as your bride screaming at her parents, "You cheapskates have ruined my whole wedding!"

If you find that you need alternate sources of financing, there are two ways to go: ask your parents to kick in, or pay for things yourself. There's nothing wrong with either option; it's become quite common to pay for your own wedding, or at least the parts of it for which no one else wants to claim responsibility, like an open bar or free-flying doves. In the end, you'll find a way to get the things you want or you'll learn that you might have to settle for something else. Dealing with overly ambitious projections, tightly squeezed budgets, demanding would-be managers, and bills that must be paid has got to be great experience for something. Oh yeah, it's called real life.

Hers
....

WEDDING CONSULTANTS

IMAGINE having at your beck and call a person whose sole reason for being is to indulge your every wedding whim. Want life-size ceramic flamingos as centerpieces? A wedding planner can hunt them down quicker than you can say, "American Express." For any bride with big dreams but no army of helpers to execute them, hiring a really good professional consultant can streamline the wedding process so that all you have to do is get yourself to the church on time. Wedding planners know who to book and when. They coordinate and oversee vendors, they supervise and cue the wedding party and music, they help with seating arrangements, and they smooth over rough spots.

Of course, hiring a consultant isn't for everyone. Some brides and their mothers would rather stick a fork in their eye than give up control of their wedding. And consultants aren't free; they represent yet another debit in your already inflated budget. But if you fall into any of the following categories, the services of a professional could be a lifesaver.

The Time-challenged. Planning a wedding is a full-time job, and if you're already gainfully employed, it's tough to shoehorn in all the necessary phone calls and in-person appointments. When you don't have a lot of time, you can make major mistakes or forget things altogether. It may be worth hiring a consultant just to avoid the fatal error of, say, getting a bar with no bartender, or neglecting to send off the deposit check for the reception hall.

The Taste-challenged. Some people were born knowing what colors go with what. If this isn't you, don't fret. A wedding consultant can act like an interior designer, helping you create the look you want for the ceremony but can't articulate. Vendors don't have time to get inside your brain and figure out what you're looking for, whereas a wedding planner is trained to pull information out of you, interpret it, and distribute it in the language a harassed florist or caterer will understand.

The Detail-challenged. Are you the type whose life falls apart when you lose your calendar? On the other end of the spectrum, do you even have a calendar? Managing the fine points of the average nuptial extravaganza can make those who aren't detail oriented miserably unhappy. It may be a huge relief to pay someone to take the minutiae off your hands. One bride who hired a professional planner was astonished at all the details he took care of, including reminding her to place an order for thank-you notes when she selected the invitations.

The Finance-challenged. How can spending money on a consultant help you save money? Because it's her job to have good relationships with established vendors, and her connections may get you lower prices or free perks. An experienced wedding planner knows how much things should cost and can bargain for fair prices, negotiate contracts in your favor, and avoid overtime charges.

The Distance-challenged. Planning an out-of-town wedding? Good luck. It's hard enough to organize a major social event, but when you have to travel hundreds of miles to book a reception hall, the logistical difficulties soar to the level of nightmares. Hiring an out-of-town consultant means that she'll do much of the long-distance legwork for you, and you can work with her primarily by telephone.

The Family-challenged. A consultant is the equivalent of Switzerland in a wedding. She is a neutral party whose job is to solve problems without taking sides. She can negotiate disputes that may arise among family members and shoulder the burden of trying to accommodate everyone's specific needs. While temporary insanity can make parents and in-laws lose sight of the fact that this is your wedding, a consultant will never forget it. She is there to make sure your fiancé and you are the king and the queen of the prom.

· His ·

WEDDING CONSULTANTS

Most guys have no idea that wedding consultants exist, but once the concept is explained to us, we wonder why we didn't hire one sooner—like the instant we popped the question. Basically, a wedding consultant (coordinator, planner, organizer—they have many titles) will find out what kind of wedding you and your fiancée want and how much you can afford to spend, then she'll go off and make everything happen. I mean everything, from the place, date, and time to itinerary management at the reception.

With a wedding consultant on the job, you can give your input on the things you care about without lifting a finger to help with the things you don't. Aside from registering for gifts, which you'll never be able to avoid doing, all you have to do is jump when the wedding consultant says so.

As with any service, you'll have to do some research before you hire someone. It's easy to go with a recommendation from a friend or parent, but you'll probably be more comfortable with your choice of wedding consultant if you solicit feedback from previous clients about his or her work. When you meet with consultants, request pictures of weddings they've run and lists of references. Take time to call the references, and don't just ask, "So, how did you like Kitty Coordinator?" Dig a bit deeper into the situation with questions like:

"Was Kitty a good listener?"

"At any point, did you feel like she was *too* controlling?"

"Do you think you saved money using her?"

"Did your wedding reflect your personalities or hers?"

"What did the rest of your family think of her?"

Once you settle on a consultant who seems to fit your style, you still have some preliminary work to do. Most wedding consultants, like realtors or brokers of any kind, don't always work with the entire range of available vendors. In other words, when you go into a consultant's office without having seen a single reception hall on your own, the consultant will probably show you the four or five he or she usually works with. The perfect reception hall may not even deal with wedding consultants, or, if they do, they may not deal regularly with the one you've chosen. You may end up missing out on the best space for your wedding simply because you didn't know it existed.

I suggest you do at least some research into local sites and vendors so

SEVEN SURVIVAL TIPS FOR HANDLING PUSHY WEDDING CONSULTANTS

1. Since the groom is assumed to be an absolute imbecile in wedding matters, ask your fiancée to express your concerns about the twelve-foot tall cake.
2. Compliment your consultant often. Flattery will get you everywhere.
3. Begin any complaints positively: "The fire dancers are great, but wouldn't a traditional band be less... frightening?"
4. Never say "No" to a control freak. "I'll think about it" works better.
5. Wedding consultants regularly deal with mothers of the brides, so they eat punks like you for breakfast. In other words, threats will get you nowhere.
6. Every once in a while, throw in "That's not what our other wedding consultant said!"
7. There is one threat that works with consultants: mention the word "elope."

you'll have some knowledge to draw upon when you sit down with your consultant. Of course, you can't search every possible corner of the earth for fear of what you're missing (especially if you're getting married out of town), and if you plan on getting married in a relatively small town, chances are the wedding consultant knows and works with all the best vendors in the area. It never hurts to do independent research, though, even if it feels like you're doing some of the work you thought you hired a consultant to do for you.

If you get a great consultant, you'll wonder how you could have pulled off your wedding alone. However, if you're very unlucky, your future in-laws will do the consultant hiring and you may be stuck with the queen mother of all control freaks. If this is your plight, I suggest you liberally use the seven survival tips I offer. Beyond that, remember what Marine recruits tell each other at Parris Island: What doesn't kill you makes you stronger.

· Hers ·

GUEST LIST

As you plan your wedding, there will be many times when you're tempted to tear your hair out by the roots and scream, "Who's getting married, anyway?" Putting together your guest list may be one of those occasions.

Here's what usually happens. While still glowing with newly engaged excitement, you sit down with your husband-to-be and write down the names of all your friends, close co-workers, and immediate family members. Then you start saying things like, "Well, if we invite your friend Nancy, we can't invite my friend Andrew, but we'll have to invite Nancy's roommate's friend Dan. So Sally's roommate will have to come too. And there's no way my aunt Fuscia will come unless my cousin Bitsy comes, and if we invite your uncle Ned there's no way he won't tell Great-uncle Elmo, who probably won't come, but if he does he'll need wheelchair access and a macrobiotic meal."

After you wind your way through this first maze, you may have about a hundred names, which seems reasonable. You send copies of the list to your mother and your mother-in-law-to-be, with a cheerful note, "Let us know if we've forgotten anyone!" When you open the envelope that comes back, a scroll unrolls to the floor. You're now up to about four hundred names, because it's absolutely imperative that your parents' entire office staffs, yoga instructors, and twice-removed relatives share in your big day. One new bride told me that her mother insisted on inviting all her cousins—even the ones she didn't like or had never met—simply because the groom's mother was inviting cousins and they were sharing the cost of the wedding.

Next, you start getting phone calls. Everyone, from people you went to camp with when you were ten to old enemies from high school, telephones to congratulate you and fish around for an invitation. Your co-workers all let you know how much they look forward to coming to the wedding. The guest list balloons to five hundred names, and you haggle, you negotiate, you knock it back to a still daunting three hundred. You think, "I'll have no clue who all these people are smiling at me as I walk down the aisle." Then you think, "Wow! I'm gonna rake in a lot of loot!"

The invitations go out. The RSVPs come in. Some people have written, "Mr. and Mrs. Smith will attend," and some have written, "Mr. and Mrs. Smith will not attend." Others, helpfully, have written, "Mr. and Mrs. Smith (and Betty and Lisa and Edward and Johnny) will attend. Can't wait to see you! P.S. Johnny will need a highchair." When all is said and done, the number of probable attendees has crept back up toward 350.

How can you keep a firm grip on your final guest list? Well, one perfectly acceptable option is to specify on your invitations that children are not included. If anyone asks or complains about why you haven't invited children or unknown guests, be honest. "Our budget is pretty tight. But I really want you there." Let them know your wedding is going to be small, you have two families to accommodate, and it's impossible to invite everyone.

Another way to keep attendance down is to hold your wedding on a holiday weekend or out of town. Alice deliberately planned to be married on the Sunday after the Fourth of July, reasoning that she would only lose those people she and her fiancé weren't really close to. She invited 210 people, and only 140 came. Another option is to underinvite—in other words, if your budget will allow you to have 150 guests, formally invite only 125. They say you can count on a 70 percent positive response, so you'll have plenty of room for guests to bring other guests.

Sit down and talk with your parents—and your fiancé—about who you really want to be with on your wedding day. When you look back on this day, who will you regret not seeing? Have you invited people you won't be able to identify in five years? And, while you're absolutely right to believe that those you want at your wedding should be people you both adore, try to reconcile yourself to the fact that you probably won't get the guest list just exactly where you want it.

Come up with a system that seems fair and stick with it at all cost: Kara, her parents, and her fiancé's parents were splitting the cost of the wedding three ways. They determined how many guests they could afford to invite, and each group was allowed a third of the total. It's all too easy for a guest list to bloat like Wonder bread in the rain, but do try to respect the wishes of your loved ones. It's a big day for them, too.

· *His* ·
GUEST LIST

SOON after your engagement, you'll begin forming your wedding guest list. You'll actually finalize it on the morning of the wedding. The reason guest lists are so shifty is that each name represents a person who is connected to and affected by friendships or kinships to other people who may or may not be on the list. The minute you write down a name on your guest list, such as Fred who works in the office next to you, a whole list of related names must be added, like every person you've ever worked with. When Fred says he and his wife can't make it, you're still stuck with all the work friends you didn't want to invite in the first place.

The etiquette of inviting co-workers to your wedding could be the subject of an entire book, but basically, it's standard to invite your immediate supervisor, plus those co-workers with whom you are friendly outside of work. One groom narrowed his guest list to those people he'd seen socially within the last year. The exception to this rule is if you work in a very tiny office, because you may then have to invite everyone or no one at all. One option is to send around an open invitation to your wedding, but stipulate that people must let you know by a certain date if they will attend.

Your genealogical chart entangles you in another web of names whom you can't possibly snub, from great-uncles you haven't seen in years to cousins you've never met. When you add on your parents' friends, their kids, and their kids' dates, you end up with an impossibly intricate, interwoven, unstable matrix of people, only a dozen of whom you actually want to see on your wedding day.

Trimming the guest list is difficult, since removing one card may cause the whole house to collapse. It's best to go to the caterer with your maximum possible guest list and get estimates of the cost per plate at 100 percent, 80 percent, and 60 percent of that total number. Once you do this, some simple math will tell you what you (or the bride's parents) can afford. Then you can begin weeding out names in earnest in order to bring the list down to a target number, give or take twenty or so guests.

It's a good idea to send out a round of invitations eight weeks in advance, and then, since many people will RSVP "no" right away, send out another round of invitations to those you didn't initially have room for a week later. This sort of A-list and B-list system may seem crass, but it's really just a way of making sure that the opportunity to attend will be given to as many of your nearest and dearest as you can possibly afford.

Guest list–making time is a good time to get really organized. Put all your guests' names on index cards, one card each for singles (with guests), for couples, and for families. These cards become tangible representations of the people in your life, but, unlike real life, you can move these card people around and put them exactly where you want them. First, arrange the cards along lines of acquaintance, such as Mom's side of the family, friends from college, or the church social group, so you can easily see if you've missed anyone. If one of your friends is being a jerk, stick pins through his card, or torch it with a lighter. He won't know the difference, but it will give you a great deal of satisfaction.

Few things in your wedding will be more useful than these index cards.

Want to add a few guests? Add a few more cards. Want to know how many gifts you'll get? Count your cards. Arranging your seating chart? Place compatible cards together. Use this system to help you limit the guests your parents can invite by simply giving them a certain number of cards to fill out. When you're reasonably sure you have a final guest list, the cards will act as a failsafe checklist to make sure all your invitations get out. Ditto for when the responses come in and you need to have an accurate guest count.

You may find playing with index cards to be a lot more rewarding than dealing with some of the actual guests. In fact, when guests get particularly annoying—for instance, when they bother you by complaining about the ten-minute drive from the ceremony to the reception hall—those cards will really come in handy. Take the card that corresponds to the unruly guest and find a sharp pair of scissors. I'll leave you to figure out what to do next.

· *Hers* ·

INVITATIONS

F<small>OR</small> many couples, ordering and addressing the invitations can be one of the most difficult parts of making wedding arrangements. First of all, if something goes wrong with the invitations, it can affect the execution of the whole wedding. Ever hear the one about the couple who sent out four hundred invitations embossed in gold leaf—with the wrong date?

Second, stylistic differences frequently arise. For instance, Rose and her fiancé, Harry, fought for months over their invitations because Harry wanted something very simple, high quality, and formal, whereas Rose wanted something less proper.

Third, determining the wording on wedding invitations can lead to real-life family feuds with devastating consequences. Most etiquette books say an invitation should read:

Mr. and Mrs. Sample
cordially invite you to celebrate the marriage of their daughter
Sally Sample

to John Doe, Jr.
son of Mr. and Mrs. Doe

But what if your parents are divorced? Then you have to say,

Mr. Sample and Mrs. Ex-Sample
cordially invite... etc.

And if one or both is remarried, here comes World War III over whether new wives and husbands get their names on the invitations.

Now what if the groom's parents are paying for a good part of the ceremony? Dollars to doughnuts, they'll want their names to have better real estate on the invitations. Marcy found this out the hard way: her in-laws left a scathing message on her machine when they received their invitations in the mail and noticed their names weren't on them. What they wanted was something like:

Mr. Sample and Mrs. New Sample
and Mr. and Mrs. Ex-Sample with a New Name
cordially invite you to celebrate the wedding of their daughter
Sally Sample
to John Doe
son of Mr. and Mrs. Doe
and Mr. and Mrs. I Got All the Doe in the Divorce

At this point, you have to reconcile yourself to either having an invitation the size of a legal pad, or running onto the backside of the card. Unattractive as that prospect may seem, possibly the worst scenario is if the bride and groom are paying for the wedding themselves and, heaven forbid, want their invitations to come from themselves. Something like:

Sally and John
cordially invite you to celebrate their marriage

This will go over about as well as refusing to have your parents give you away. If your parents truly care about either of these issues, you'd better pack it in now. There's just no way to win.

On the upside, some brides have used invitation subterfuge to handle deeper wedding issues between the two families involved. Consider the cases of two brides who solved their problems the same way. Amanda's family wanted her invitations to say, "Reception at 1:00 P.M.," since that was when they told the reception hall the party would start. Amanda's fiancé's family wanted the invitations to read, "Reception at 12:30 P.M.," since the ceremony would end at 11:30 and they felt people would arrive at the reception hall early. The men in Julie's family were adamantly opposed to renting tuxedos for her wedding, and refused to come at all if the invitations said, "Black Tie Only." Her fiancé's family insisted that the wedding be black tie. After months of fighting, both brides secretly had two sets of invitations printed. Amanda's parents, friends, and relatives received invitations reading "Reception at 1:00 P.M." while her fiancé's family received invitations stating "Reception at 12:30 P.M." Julie's parents and their friends got "Black Tie Optional" and her fiancé's parents and their friends got "Black Tie Only."

The interesting thing about planning a wedding is that you begin to realize how insensitive you've been in the past regarding your soon-to-be-wed friends. You regret every time you bought a gift that wasn't on the registry, and you recall, with excruciating clarity, the times you neglected to send back an RSVP card because you were just too busy. Well, it's payback time. You'd think that if you send people a self-addressed stamped envelope they'd be able to check off a simple "Yes, will attend" or "No, won't attend" and pop the thing in the mail, but for some reason people either procrastinate sending in their RSVPs or think that they already did, when the card's still lying under a pile of mail somewhere.

If you've written up index cards of each guest you've invited, now you can put a check mark on each one as those guests RSVP. Then, as the wedding date gets closer, give the cards of those who haven't responded to your mother or your maid of honor and make her play repo man. Many brides don't feel comfortable tracking down tardy RSVPs themselves, but it's important to find out rather than assume a guest is coming or not. If you or someone else absolutely can't call, act as if the guest is coming and make sure you've set aside food and a seat. Better to pay for an extra meal than to have a guest show up with no place to sit.

· *His* ·

INVITATIONS

SITTING in a card store choosing wedding invitations out of a big binder is about the most fun two people can have with their clothes on. Okay, I'm lying. But you have to do it, so you might as well look on the bright side.

Okay, there is no bright side. In truth, choosing wedding invitations is quite frustrating, because while you'll be perfectly happy with the third sample you see—which looks an awful lot like the first, twenty-fifth, and thousandth samples—your fiancée won't be content until she's seen every invitation in every book in every card store in town. As a result, most men end up saying, "Honey, whatever you choose is fine with me," which leads her to start the "You don't care about our wedding and I'm doing all the work" argument.

But wait, it gets worse. You've neglected to give your valuable input on the color of ink, engraving vs. embossing, rounded corners vs. beveled edges, natural tones vs. bright whites, calligraphy for the envelopes, calligraphy for the envelopes inside the envelopes inside the envelopes, and last but not least, the picture on the stamps. You will gamely suggest the Elvis stamp, citing the

King's numerous musings on the nature of love, or perhaps the Frankenstein stamp, noting that the monster was really a tender being whose motives were completely misunderstood. Of course, you will be denied. The envelope of a wedding invitation is no place for your personality to shine through. It's a dove, flower, heart, or love stamp, and that's the end of the discussion.

When your fiancée recognizes how useless you are in the invitation arts, she may give you something you can actually handle: directions. Accept this mission and pursue it with vigor. Fuel up the car, set your odometer to zero, put new batteries in your voice recorder, and hit the road. You'll end up with three hours of recorded directions on how to get to your wedding and reception sites, the rehearsal dinner, and five local hotels from every possible compass direction. You'll note every curve, traffic light, road fork, and 7-Eleven along the way, and measure your distances in tenths of a mile.

Sucking down a Slurpee, you'll input the information on your laptop, pleased with your day's work and the fact that you did it the way it was meant to be done. One man, one job. Mission accomplished. Then your fiancée will round off your carefully measured distances, reduce your masterpiece to one page, and have it printed without showing you until the deed is done. Women can be so cruel.

If you're planning an entire holiday weekend for your guests, you probably won't be satisfied with one invitation in the mail. Andy and Felicia sent out consecutive packets of information. Those traveling from far away were sent a "save this date" card warning them to keep Memorial Day weekend free and reserve hotel rooms for the occasion early. (These cards are becoming increasingly popular and are often ordered at the same time as the invitations and thank-you notes.)

Then, Andy and Felicia sent two more packages, one with the formal wedding invitation, and one with a more casual invitation to some fun prewedding events—a golf outing and an amusement park trip for everyone instead of a rehearsal dinner for a few. Finally, a few weeks before the big weekend, they sent out directions and reminder agendas to keep everyone informed about what was going to happen.

Of course, you don't have to use the postal service to get your message across. Thanks to the Internet, you can deliver wedding information through your very own Web site. One service, www.weddingrsvp.com, helps you create your own nuptial home page with a guest e-mail response section, directions to the ceremony, and even information about your guest registry that you'd be embarrassed to put anywhere else.

Maybe someday, to the delight of men everywhere, we won't have to send out formal wedding invitations at all, just nicely designed e-mails with digital picture files attached. Everyone will drive to the ceremony using the Global Positioning Satellite coordinates you've downloaded. Of course, your fiancée will still edit them first. Some things will never change.

· Hers ·

SEATING CHART

WHEN you think back on all the weddings you've attended in your lifetime, you're most likely to remember either heinous displays of tastelessness, hilarious things that went wrong, or the dreadful/terrific strangers whose company you shared for hours. Comparing notes after a wedding we recently attended, Dave and I were astonished at how much fun we'd had. Yes, the food was good and the band was lively, but what it really came down to was the fact that we were seated at a table where we truly enjoyed meeting all the strangers we were seated with.

Most wedding planning books include a page that you're supposed to use as a worksheet for completing your seating arrangements. What they fail to tell you, however, is that you should Xerox at least twenty copies of it, because you'll be arranging, and rearranging, and rearranging, and then rearranging some more, up until mere minutes before the ceremony starts. The only reason the rearranging stops then is because you've closeted yourself in a small room with one or two bridesmaids, your dress, a curling iron, and a lot of makeup, and you're simply unavailable to the legions of whiners who've been deluging you for months with ultimatums like, "You can't seat me at the same table with Aunt Margie. She talks when she eats, spits when she talks, and I sat next to her at the last wedding and swore I'd never do it again."

When making seating arrangements, there's a whole gamut of factors to take into consideration, including political beliefs, personal hygiene, race, religion, marital status, and recent life crises. After writing each guest's name on an index card, Dave and I attached a Post-it note detailing any restricting personal behaviors or preferences. For example, the card for our friend Don read, "Talks politics incessantly. Do not seat with Democrats. Do not seat with Allison, who works at a Planned Parenthood clinic." The card for my great-uncle Franklin read, "Has numerous questionable health concerns. Do not seat with anyone in the medical profession." We then arranged the cards to simulate table assignments, and interchanged them as necessary.

SEVEN SURVIVAL TIPS FOR MAKING THE PERFECT SEATING CHART

1. No requests. What the bride says goes.
2. Don't try to set single friends up by seating them together. Matchmaking is a delicate art that requires more time than you have at your wedding.
3. Give guests at least one partner whom they're comfortable sitting with.
4. Seat fun people far away from the dance floor, so they can gather reluctant dancers on their way to it.
5. Unless you want a food fight, a children's table is a bad idea.
6. Go for interesting social combinations, and try to mix friends from different areas of your lives.
7. Don't let a wedding etiquette book dictate who sits with you at your table. Surround yourself with the people you enjoy the most.

Due to our obsessive arranging, the glue wore completely off the Post-its. We went to bed one night having left the ultimate seating arrangement spread out in the middle of the living room floor. Unfortunately, during the night the cat did wheelies through all those little scraps of paper. We took a deep breath and started over from scratch.

If you have the time and patience, you may want to assign guests to a specific *seat* — not just a table — using preset placecards. This is a great way to get those people whom you think will get along sitting next to each other, not just across from each other. Be forewarned that this may backfire — one bride was astonished to see people at her reception running around madly rearranging placecards because they didn't like where they had been put.

Finally, to avoid major wedding guest warfare, go for larger tables as opposed to small ones. One bride made the mistake of having tables for four at her reception, and she still gets complaints from couples who were imprisoned for the duration of the nuptials with another couple whom they couldn't stand.

· *His* ·

SEATING CHART

I'M sure Wendy suggests a rational, methodical way to get through the odious task of filling out the seating chart for the reception; however, I have a technique that avoids all that boring compromising and nasty yelling. It's time to play a game I call "Who gets stuck sitting next to Aunt Agnes?" You'll need the following equipment for maximum f-u-n:

One (1) groom

One (1) bride

No (0) mothers-in-law

One (1) Twister mat

A bunch (???) of index cards

The index cards are the same ones you prepared in the chapter "The Guest List," one for each single guest, couple, or family you invite. The spots on the Twister mat represent the tables at your reception. To play, follow these simple steps:

1. Put a table number on each spot

2. Shuffle index cards thoroughly

3. Stand in middle of Twister mat

4. Throw cards in air

5. Where they land is where they sit

To eliminate any show of favoritism for pesky best friends and family patriarchs, I encourage you to use the built-in Twister color coding scheme. Blue spots mean tables close to the bride and groom. Green means these guests get priority seating and won't starve to death before they get served their dinner. Yellow offers a lovely view of the ladies' room. And red, of course, gets a faceful of wedding band amplifiers.

In a Utopian society, the Twister selection process would be the ideal alternative to the real-life negotiations and sacrifices involved in the actual seating arrangement process. At the very least, random selection could result in an explosive combination of guests, which would probably create a more interesting wedding overall.

Alas, for most engaged couples the traditional, painful seating technique most often prevails. Begin by seating together people who know and like each other, and do the same with people who have similar interests and personalities. Place family with family, young with young, old with old. Put the wedding party at the head table, family nearby, college and high school friends near the band. Yawn.

When you arrange seats the old-fashioned way, there is one meager source of enjoyment: the leftover table. That's the one populated with grumpy old men no one likes, weird single friends who don't play well with others, odd people from work you weren't sure you were going to invite, folks who smell funny, and last-minute invitees. Watching the leftovers interact is like luck-ing into ringside seats at the circus. You may be witness to several hours of uncomfortable silence, loud disagreements, inappropriate touching, or even a food fight. Who knows, maybe a freakish love story will unfold. Your old-maid aunt may not be so grumpy after all when a Romeo in platform shoes makes goo-goo eyes at her from around the centerpiece.

·Hers·

PLEASING EVERYONE

DURING the initial stage of planning a wedding, every bride thinks she's special. By this I mean every bride thinks she's going to succeed in hosting the party of her dreams. Little does the bride know she's really charged with hosting the party of two hundred other people's dreams. Her role is to act as a clearinghouse for the needs of every guest and participant, and she must reconcile all these needs so that her wedding is a composite event that makes everyone happy.

You will learn this when you make a unilateral decision only to get a message on your answering machine that says something like, "I just heard the bridesmaids' dresses are going to be lilac, but you're going to have to pick another color. You know how purple aggravates my asthma."

You will learn this when your mother puts her foot down about something while your future mother-in-law simultaneously puts down the opposite foot.

You will learn this when you find out that the one thing you really feel strongly about is the one thing your fiancé feels equally and opposingly strongly about.

You will learn this when your plans are at an absolute impasse because no one around you is willing to compromise.

And every time you hear the words, "I know this is your special day" you will develop a reflexive shudder because that phrase is always followed by the word "but" and an ultimatum.

Depending on what kind of person you are, there are two ways you can react to the demands of others. One is to realize, early on, that there is no way you can make everyone happy and simply plow ahead with your plans while ignoring distress calls from the peanut gallery. The other is to be like the willow and try to bend wherever you can while repeating the mantra, "In _____ days I will be married. In _____ days I will be married." In any event, the only good news about wanting to please everyone is that everyone who's been through planning a wedding likens it to childbirth: you remember afterward that there was pain, but the feeling itself disappears without a trace.

· *His* ·

PLEASING EVERYONE

YOUR mother wants your wedding to be held within three hundred miles of her home because her psychic told her she should never fly. Because of her skin condition, your aunt has requested a special meal of white bread, peanut butter, and boiled cabbage at the reception. It seems like the minute you pop the question, the requests for special treatment started rolling in from the four corners of the earth.

Every day the list gets longer and more annoying. It's only a matter of time until your mother demands the opposite of what your fiancée's mother demanded last week, and *blam*, you've got a situation on your hands. This is the point when eloping starts to sound like a pretty good idea.

Your and your bride's parents have a familial and a financial interest in your wedding, so to a certain extent, they're allowed to exercise their opinions. But why do other people feel they have a right to dictate what you do at your wedding? Despite the title of this chapter, it's simply impossible to please everyone, but, like any wedding gift, you can return the guilt everyone lays on you. Show demanding people the error of their ways by asking them the following questions in order. Proceed to the next question only if a particular guest doesn't throw up his hands and walk away.

THE "PUTTING SELFISH GUESTS IN THEIR PLACE" FLOWCHART

Why do you feel you have the right to dictate what I do at my own wedding?

↓

Do you think it's possible for you to live without a) standing with us at the altar b) a fondue station or c) requesting "The Chicken Dance?"

↓

Knowing that I'm one annoyance away from grabbing a rifle and climbing a tower, are you sure you want to add this little bit of pressure to me now?

↓

Well golly, your concerns seem valid. Mind if I call my lawyer about this?

↓

Do you still want to come to our wedding?

↓

Would you like me to smack you firmly on the back of the head?

·*Hers*·

DECISION MAKING

WHEN Dave and I planned our wedding, I think things would have been much easier if only I had listened to him from the beginning. From day one of the engagement, he made it very clear that he cared very much about getting married, and about having an open bar for our wedding guests. Now, I don't know how I did it, but from that I somehow concluded that he also cared about what kind of flowers we'd have at the reception, what kind of food we'd serve, what time of year and what time of day we would be married, who would officiate, and what my dress would look like.

What was I thinking? He had made his priorities perfectly clear, and yet I still labored under the impression that the process of planning our wedding was to include joint decision making. Many very intelligent women make this mistake, and you can save yourself long months of agony by using this easy-to-follow translation guide.

What you say	**What he thinks**
Honey, shall we serve chicken and rice or chicken and pasta?	*Whatever goes with beer.*
Who did you like better — band #1 or DJ #7?	*Whichever goes with beer.*
Do you think the trailing clematis overshadows the wild orchids in the centerpieces?	*If there's enough beer, no one will notice.*

While you may think these are questions of the utmost importance and the happiness of your guests depends on the answers, the real question is whether there is any way to make your fiancé give a hoot about them. I know you want to include him; I know you want him to enjoy the day. But let's face it: he'll be thrilled with the wedding as long as a) at the end of it he's officially married to you and b) the only tears you shed are tears of happiness.

Rather than wasting your energy bringing your husband into the decision-making process, you may want to get help from someone who really cares: your mother or your mother-in-law. If your fiancé's interest in trailing clematis rates a 1 on the caring scale, the interest level of a mom starts around 206.

· *His* ·

DECISION MAKING

As a single man, you're used to making decisions, but you usually make them solo. It's easy to go from "I just got paid" to "I think I'll buy an enormous stereo," and from "I could eat a horse" to ordering a large pepperoni pizza. But by putting a diamond ring on your beloved's finger, you have effectively shifted some of your autonomy to her. That means she has a 50 percent say in where your paycheck goes, and this year, you can bet it's not going anywhere near an electronics store.

Mutual decision making is certainly not a bad thing. In fact, as you and your wife-to-be get better at it, you'll end up making more satisfying decisions together than you ever did alone. Preparing for a wedding is essentially decision-making boot camp. Each drill is designed to test and hone your skills for the real-life decisions you'll be making as husband and wife. Choosing your wedding site will give you the basic experience you need to buy a house; determining a coordinated color scheme for the flowers, table linens, and wedding party apparel will teach you how to make home decorating decisions together. And deciding on the roles your parents will play in your wedding is just a prelude to managing their influence as grandparents of your first child.

Decision making as a team may be difficult at first; it may take a long time, involve a few arguments, and spawn many more exhaustive discussions than you feel are necessary. Because you're still in training, though, nobody expects you to get it right the first time, so you don't have to treat every decision like it's the one factor that will make or break your wedding.

But you do have to care. At least to the extent that you will talk about an issue that's important to your fiancée, even if you're ultimately asking her to make a decision about it herself. One prospective groom, Ron, searched his soul and figured out that only three wedding-related things were truly important to him: the bride, the place, and the band. When his fiancée, Valerie, asked him to come with her to register for china patterns, he said that whatever she picked would be fine. An argument ensued. After a heated discussion, Ron finally explained that he had no relevant experience and no taste for dishes, and therefore he would be nothing but a burden to Valerie at the store. He expressed his vague impression that plain is better than patterns, and promised to play a greater role in making decisions for which he felt more qualified. Valerie registered for gifts with her mother; Ron stayed home and watched the ball game; and everybody was happy.

All Valerie really wanted was for Ron to show an interest, and once she recognized that dishes weren't his forte—and received reassurance that he wouldn't complain about her choices—she found someone else to help her make dish-related decisions. This is a valuable lesson. If you feel you're not qualified to make a particular decision, research it or suggest someone else who can help. But discuss it either way, and don't assume your wife will deal with it on her own. Remember, it's your wedding too, and your voice should be heard.

THE UNAVOIDABLE, UNANTICIPATED CRISIS

LET'S say you are that rare well-adjusted bride who understands that life in general is unreliable, and that you may have to cope with a best man who's too drunk to give his toast, or a freak blizzard in August. There's a big difference, however, between such minor tears in the fabric of your wedding and a crisis that threatens to send the whole thing up in flames.

It's the difference between a funny story ("The ushers tied so many condoms to the getaway car that they melted in the engine") and a story about the wedding-that-almost-never-was. Stacy, for instance, is almost legally blind, and her contact lenses tore an hour before the wedding as she was getting dressed. Since she literally wouldn't have been able to see her way down the aisle, she was forced to find an optometrist who could fit her with an emergency pair of glasses. As if that weren't challenge enough, Stacy's fiancé had borrowed her car. So, half-dressed in her wedding gear, Stacy hijacked a neighbor on his way to pick up some groceries and made him drive her thirty minutes to the nearest one-hour eyeglasses store.

My point is, it's common with weddings for a crisis of seemingly monumental proportions to emerge out of nowhere. The crisis is often so bizarre that you're tempted to believe a higher power is sending you a message not to get married. It's usually something so weird you couldn't have made it up if you'd tried.

What makes the unavoidable, unanticipated crisis so frustrating is that it is, by definition, both unavoidable and unanticipated. You could worry nonstop about all the things that could happen, but even then the one thing you didn't worry about is the thing that will happen. Telling a bride not to worry about her own wedding is like telling a snowman not to melt.

But this is supposed to be one of the happiest times of your life. Do you really want to spend it consumed with anxiety? Worrying never prevents or solves a problem, it just makes you miserable. Erin went to at least thirty separate stores in search of the perfect wedding dress. She took six months to find it, and had four fittings to make sure it was perfectly tailored. But right before she was scheduled to pick up the dress from the shop—two days before her wedding—the shop burned down to the ground. I'm not kidding; it was in the papers.

The good news is, usually a crisis of this sort only happens once. The bad news is, at the time, it seems absolutely insurmountable. How on earth could Erin find the perfect replacement dress, tailored to fit, in less than forty-eight hours? Answer: she couldn't. But she could find a dress that was good enough and that fitted well enough, give or take a safety pin or two.

Whatever your personal crisis turns out to be, I promise you'll survive it. You may even laugh about it eventually. So do whatever you can to make your wedding run smoothly, and when that crazy disaster rears up out of nowhere and smacks you over the head, let yourself be flabbergasted and appalled. Then—deal with it. There's really nothing you can't handle.

· *His* ·

THE UNAVOIDABLE, UNANTICIPATED CRISIS

CONSIDER the story of Tucker and Kate, two of the most organized people you'll ever meet. In planning their wedding, they had made detailed plans for every possible contingency. If it was sunny, their reception would be held outside in an elegant garden; if it rained they would move inside to a spacious ballroom. They provided a floor plan and written instructions for each parent and member of the bridal party so everyone would know exactly where to stand and what to do when.

A week before the wedding they were good to go. That's when they got a call from Father Cunningham. "Yes, ah, Kate? I'm afraid I have some bad news. It seems I've made the mistake of double booking your wedding day. You see, I had already committed to marrying another couple the evening of June twenty-fourth by the time I got the call from you [a year ago], and my assistant never pointed out the conflict in my engagement book until today. I'm dreadfully sorry, but I can't perform your wedding."

Have you ever cursed out a priest? Kate wasn't sure what type of sin that would be, but she came close to committing it right over the phone. Worse still, Father Cunningham had already checked around town to find a replacement priest for the twenty-fourth, but in the height of the wedding season, he found nobody who was available on such short notice. He offered to perform the wedding an hour earlier or an hour later, but the thought of calling up 250 guests and saying, "Sorry, can you please arrive an hour late?" sent shivers up the spine of ultraorganized Kate. Exasperated, she said she and Tucker would work it out themselves and hung up the phone.

When Tucker heard the news, he simmered for a minute or two, then started brainstorming solutions. "What if we look up churches in the phone book? What if we hire a justice of the peace, then get the marriage blessed by Father Cunningham later? What if...?" Meanwhile, Kate was in tears. She kept asking over and over, "How could he just cancel on us like that? I worked so hard and now the wedding's ruined. Why is life so unfair?"

Of course, not all brides react this way, but when faced with the unavoidable, unanticipated crisis, many will, maybe even your own fiancée. To most men, this way of thinking seems self-pitying and unproductive. Like Tucker, you may wonder how Kate could just sit there and feel sorry for herself when there was so big a problem to be solved and so little time to solve it. For many men, anger is the first and only reaction to crisis, followed by a need to solve it quickly and get on with our lives. Two hours after the problem first arose, we've moved on to "Did somebody say... McDonald's?"

But for most women, especially brides who have been dreaming of their wedding day since they can remember having dreams, the reaction is less cut-and-dried. An important fact that Tucker learned, and that most married men learn sooner or later, is that many women initially need to ponder and talk about the misery of a situation. This may take some time. If you're faced with a major crisis in the midst of your wedding plans, you will eventually have to figure out the best solution, but here are some suggestions that will help you deal with your fiancée:

- Talk with her about the problem, and allow her to feel that it's not just maddening, stupid, and unlucky, but also heartbreaking and sad.

- Don't tell her not to worry and then insist on solving the problem yourself. She wants to be involved in the solution, and she doesn't necessarily want to be insulated or protected from the pain.

- Touch her. Long hugs and soothing backrubs or footrubs are great for emotional pain and frustration.

- There's a great book entitled *Wedding Nightmares*. Sharing it with your fiancée is guaranteed to make your problem seem like a dance through the daisies.

And to avoid the unavoidable unanticipated crisis altogether?

- Double-check your officiant's wedding schedule *right now.*

- Sacrifice a live chicken to Fribble, the god of smooth-running weddings.

- Sell everything you own and hire two photographers, two florists, etc.

- Carry a rabbit's foot for the duration of the wedding planning process, and eat Lucky Charms for breakfast, lunch, and dinner.

· *Hers* ·

Last-Minute Arrangements

MOST wedding books offer you a cheery little introduction that says something like,

> *There's absolutely no reason you should be stressed out and overwhelmed in the weeks right before your wedding. The secret lies in not leaving everything to the last minute—a smart bride plans ahead! In the next 532 pages, we'll show you how to get all the planning out of the way early, so that, during the final countdown, you can relax and enjoy spending time with your friends and family members.*

What a load of hooey. Because if you follow the instructions in these books religiously—dotting your i's, crossing your t's, and dutifully planning ahead, two weeks before the wedding you'll still end up mired in chapter 35, entitled something like, "Whoops! All the Things You Forgot to Do."

The fact is, no matter how efficient and organized you are, the last few weeks before your wedding will be a blur of little details. You can always spot a bride-

Six Things Brides Think They Have to Do Before the Wedding

1. Become a size 6.
2. Get Cameron Diaz's nose.
3. Grow five inches of hair to put in an elegant chignon.
4. Cultivate stiletto nails.
5. Develop a flawless complexion.
6. Acquire perfect teeth.

about-to-be: she's the one walking around in a trance, mumbling things like, "Pick up bridesmaids' shoes. Pick up rings. Wrap gifts for bridal party. Find home for cat while on honeymoon." Part of it is because there are certain things you just can't do until the last minute. You have to have a last dress fitting, for example, right before the wedding, in case you've succeeded in starving off those last five pounds. You have to get a haircut and highlights and have your nails done, for heaven's sake, and you have to buy special wedding stockings. You have to finalize the guest list and seating chart, since some folks (probably on your in-laws' list) decided to wait until the last second to RSVP.

Most of us have to squeeze in all those appointments while holding down our regular full-time job. Plus we realize all the things we've taken for granted at other people's weddings. Those birdseed sachets don't just show up at the reception: somebody has to buy the birdseed and the netting and the ribbons and fashion it all into two hundred little baggies, and that somebody is probably you. If you don't put together a basket of toiletries and a dish of potpourri to put in the bathroom for your guests, who will? Where do you suppose the ringbearer's pillow comes from? Yup—you.

The last few weeks before the wedding tend to be consumed by things you simply didn't have time to think about while you were taking care of the major plans. This is why it's a good idea to turn certain tasks over to your fiancé: jobs like applying for the marriage license and planning the honeymoon are things he won't find too distasteful.

Once he arranges the honeymoon, you may think that all you have to do is have a bag ready for the trip. But if you've changed your name, you can't get on a plane unless your driver's license and/or passport match the name on your plane ticket, and you can't change either of those until you have your marriage license. Even if you apply early for the license, it takes a while to be issued and then you have to go get the thing, which you usually put off doing because you have to apply for a license in the state where you're getting married, and if you're getting married out of town, who has time to make a special trip to get it? Once you have the license, you have 1,001 forms to fill out, because now that you're changing your driver's license and passport, you figure you should change your credit cards, bank account, social security card, and the name on your electric bill.

SIX THINGS YOU *CAN* DO BEFORE THE WEDDING

1. Lose five pounds.
2. Have your wedding-day makeup done by a professional. Get a test makeover first to avoid last-minute surprises.
3. Grow hair one inch. Hate it. Cut it. Grow it. Hate it. Cut it. Hire a stylist for the day of your wedding who will make what you've got look beautiful.
4. Get regular manicures.
5. Get regular facials.
6. Have your teeth whitened. Your dentist can do this fairly cheaply; it will take about two office visits.

Rather than fighting the fact that you will be overwhelmingly busy right before your wedding, a lot of brides-to-be simply give in to it. Taking some time off from work, even just a day or two, will go a long way toward relieving stress. You may want to try to take one day off from work each week for the three to four weeks before the wedding, or else plan to take off at least a day or two right before the event. That way, you can go from appointment to appointment with ease, cranking through the last-minute shopping, logistical arranging, and paperwork with no distractions and less anxiety.

·𝓗𝒾𝓈·

LAST-MINUTE ARRANGEMENTS

THE wedding is rapidly approaching. The invitations are out, the RSVPs are in. The place, the caterer, the photographer, the flowers, the band, and the limo are good to go. Gifts registered? Check. Tuxedo? Check. Wedding cake? Check. Marriage license: whoops!

If you don't have a license, you can't have a ceremony, and if you don't have a ceremony, your guests may want their gifts back. So grab a phone book, flip to the government agency section, and find the number for the Marriage License Bureau. Ask them how you and your fiancée can get a license quickly. They'll tell you it's easy. The two of you will have to come down to the bureau, which is conveniently located in the busiest part of town in the basement of the National Guard armory (there's no parking lot so it's best to take a bus), between the hours of 10:00 and 10:05 A.M. or 3:00 and 3:30 P.M. Monday, Tuesday, and Thursday except national holidays. Bring seventeen forms of I.D., sixty-five dollars, and, in some states, the results of your blood tests.

Once you arrive, you'll find that the woman running the place is 168 years old. After waiting in line for a brisk three or four hours, you're ready to fill out some serious paperwork in triplicate (remember carbon paper?). The clerk will then take your forms and your money and put them somewhere warm to incubate for four to six weeks, at which time they will burst from their chrysalis as a fully formed marriage license, which lays there in the bureau's OUT box until you (and only you) come pick it up.

Great! So you've finally got the marriage license. What else have you forgotten? Wedding rings! Jeez, you just finished emptying your savings account for the rock that's on your fiancée's finger, and now you have to go back to the jewelry store to buy two more rings, this time with even more tough decisions to make: gold, silver, or platinum; plain, patterned, or with inlaid stones; thick or thin; scratch-resistant or hypoallergenic. Make sure your ring fits snugly but is still comfortable. It's supposed to be on your finger for life, and you'll catch holy hell if you lose it.

Once you've ordered your rings and taken them home, you may think you're finished. Not quite, Romeo. Your fiancée will have had your ring inscribed with something romantic, and if you don't do the same for her, she'll remind you about it every anniversary until you die. Write something that sums up your undying love and have it inscribed on the inside of your fiancée's ring without her knowing it. Keep it under five words, unless you bought her two rings. Putting the wedding date on the inside of the ring is always nice, and for future reference, it's an ingenious reminder in case you forget when your anniversary is or how long you've been married.

THE WEDDING APTITUDE TEST (WAT)

You've heard of the SAT and the CAT. Now we bring you the WAT, an extremely accurate method for determining if you're ready to make key decisions regarding your wedding. Take the test separately, then compare your answers.

1. The father of the bride gives you a budget of $5,000 and says, "I threw my wedding for $50, I'll be damned if I'll pay more than $5,000 for yours." You:

   a) Accept his generous offer and look for additional funding
   b) Slip a mickey in his drink and steal his credit cards
   c) Say "Thanks, but no thanks" and pay for the whole wedding yourself
   d) Get depressed and join the Foreign Legion

2. A wedding consultant asks you how much you want to spend. You:

   a) Tell the truth and ask her to stretch every dollar
   b) Tell her it's none of her nosey little business
   c) Offer a dollar amount slightly below what you can afford
   d) Say "Oh, forget it—I knew this was a bad idea"

3. When you announce your engagement to everyone at work, Horace, the weenie from accounting, asks you when he'll get his invitation. You:

a)   Explain that you're not inviting anyone from work
b)   Tell him he'll get it when furry mole-people take over the earth
c)   Tell him you're sorry but he's not invited
d)   Fold like a lawn chair and invite him plus a guest

4. Your mother demands to be seated as far away from her ex-husband as possible. You:

a)   Shuffle the seating chart around accordingly
b)   Smile and say "okay," then seat her right next to him
c)   Tell her the seating chart's been finalized and ask her to forget her differences for one day
d)   Elope

5. Your father wants an evening wedding; your spouse's father wants it in the morning. Your mother wants it inside; your spouse's mother, outside. You:

a)   Get everyone together for a big meeting and hash out an agreement
b)   Insist on an afternoon wedding, underwater
c)   Please yourself and your spouse first, then worry about what others want
d)   Agree to throw four weddings (and possibly a funeral)

6. A week before your wedding, you learn that your photographer has died. You:

a)   Ask someone in your family to take pictures
b)   Sue the photographer's estate for emotional distress

c) Calm everyone down, make lots of phone calls, and hire someone else

d) Take the pictures yourself ("Look right here and say 'I do,' honey")

7. You've just bought the wedding rings and now you have to inscribe them. Your inscription is:

a) "I'll love you always"
b) "You got what you wanted. Happy now?"
c) "Shall I compare thee to a summer's day..."
d) "Please, God, let this be over"

If the majority of your answers were A's, your wedding aptitude is in the diplomat range. You're a good person to have around when problems need smoothing out. If you frequently answered B, you're in the misanthropic range. Not only should you stay away from key wedding arrangements, you might want to reconsider getting married. If most of your answers were C's, you're a pragmatist. You take a savvy, honest approach to everything and, for the most part, that's effective. If you answered D most often, you're in the shivering bunny range. A confidence course might help you prepare to tackle your wedding.

Bride vs. Groom

· Hers ·

POWER

WHO would you think has the most power in the wedding planning process? The logical answer would be the two people getting married. But if you believe you and your fiancé are in charge of your wedding, think again. You may be doing all the work of planning, and you may have control over certain aspects of the wedding—like choosing the underwear you'll wear that day—but in reality, a wedding is a big power pie, and everyone's trying to grab a slice.

This is done by wielding one of two tools: money or emotions. Money, for instance, buys someone the power to say, "I'm paying for this, and if you don't do it my way, I'll take my check back." Emotional blackmail allows someone to say things like, "I'll never forgive you/speak to you again if you don't do it my way" or "You'll be really embarrassed if you go with your choice instead of my recommendation." Throughout the planning of your wedding, various people—parents, in-laws, best friends, caterers—will try to take control where they can, making power plays using whatever means necessary. The first step is to identify which primary strategy is being used so you can devise the proper counterstrategy.

These examples will help you learn to spot whether money or emotion is the currency being used for barter. For each statement, mark an M if you think money is the issue, and an E if you think you're being emotionally blackmailed.

Questions

1. Your mother says, "Sweetie, I refuse to watch you spend two thousand dollars on a new wedding dress when you can wear mine for free."
2. Your wedding consultant says, "Sweetie, you really don't want hothouse orchids at every table. That's just so showy."
3. Your maid of honor says, "Sweetie, gold lamé bridesmaid dresses will flatter no one. You don't want us all to look fat, do you?"

Answers

1. *E.* Your mother doesn't give a hoot what you spend on a wedding dress, she just wants you to carry on a family tradition by wearing hers.
2. *M.* Your consultant knows you can't afford hothouse orchids plus her commission.
3. *E and M.* Your maid of honor thinks she looks lame in gold lamé *and* she can't afford it, so she gives you the one-two power punch just to be sure she gets her point across.

Once you've correctly identified a power play, you can strategize the appropriate defense. Think of it as a poker game. You've been dealt a hand of cards (given a power-play ultimatum) and your choices are as follows: fold, hold, bluff, or improve your hand.

1. *Fold.* If whatever is at stake isn't completely crucial and you don't feel like fighting about it, you can always give in and save your energy for a more important battle.

2. *Hold.* On the other hand, if you're not in the mood to be railroaded, it's always an option to say, "Fine. Don't pay for it/forgive me/speak to me again." Be prepared to accept whatever reaction you get.

3. *Bluff.* Bluffing is a variation of holding. Pretend you can deal with the consequences of holding, but be ready to suffer the embarrassment of folding if your bluff gets called.

4. *Improve your hand* with a counterplay: If money is the issue, counter with emotion. For example, your mother says, "I can't stand that drafty mansion where you want to have the reception, and I'm not going to pay for it." You should then calculate the exact cost of renting the mansion, and ask her if she's aware that she's placing a price tag of that dollar amount on her daughter's happiness.

If the power play is emotional, you can turn the threat around: "Would it be worth it to you if I wore your wedding dress but never spoke to you again?"

· *His* ·

POWER

CATCH! You've got the power ball for the briefest of moments. Its possession gives you complete control over a particular situation — in this case, your wedding. You took possession when you bought the engagement ring. But unfortunately, you tossed the power ball to your girlfriend the second she said yes to your marriage proposal.

Initially, she may let you hold the ball for a bit when big decisions are made, such as where and when your wedding will be. But you'll inevitably start dropping it by saying things like, "Hey honey, instead of flowers for the wedding ceremony, how about lots of those strings of lights shaped like chili peppers?" Once you've proven you can't be trusted with the power ball, your fiancée will hang on to it until the honeymoon.

Well, she'll *try* to hang on to it; during the wedding game, there are plenty of players looking to steal that power ball away. In the months before one recent wedding, the play-by-play went something like this:

Folks, this is turning out to be one for the books. We've seen some terrific plays out there, and there's no telling who will come out on top when those wedding bells ring. The play clock is winding down on the wedding videographer issue. And the power ball is snapped. Looks like Paul the groom is calling for his brother to do the taping with his View-cam. Nope, it's a handoff to MaryAnn the bride. She's running a call-a-professional-so-we'll-have-a-wedding-video-that-doesn't-suck play! She's at the four-hundred-, the five-hundred-, the six-hundred-dollar line. . . .

Ooooohh my! A blindside tackle by Louise the mother of the bride! She grabs the power ball and shoots up the line—Louise has completely changed the play from videography to religion. She's insisting that no daughter of hers is getting married in a Catholic church. She's got some momentum going. One look at Louise's stubborn puss and the other players are cringing away. But wait! What's the groom doing? He's standing right in Louise's way. She's gonna break him in half! What the . . . ? She's stopped in front of him. They're standing there face-to-face, both of them refusing to budge. Now who's this? Bob the father of the bride is taking Paul's side, and so are the bride's sisters and brothers . . . and there's MaryAnn, the bride herself! They're all lined up against Louise! I've never seen anything like it!

Uh-oh, now they've done it. Louise is holding the power ball out for Paul to take. It's the old "You do what you have to do, but don't expect me to come to the wedding" play. Paul grabs for the ball. He fumbles. Everyone piles on! And . . . the father of the bride comes up with the ball. He takes first down with one of the sweetest "I'm paying for most of this thing and I just took the groom's side against my own wife so now everybody's going to listen to me" plays I've ever seen.

Here's the snap. Bob fades into the pocket, and he throws a tremendous bomb . . . he's putting all his eggs in one basket here . . . there's only one eligible receiver downfield . . . it's . . . it's . . . it's . . . Kitty the wedding consultant! The ball is lodged in her two-foot-high hairdo! She's eating up yardage like a runaway locomotive! Kitty's actually grabbing other players and taking them along—the photographer—the caterer—the florist—MaryAnn—she's carrying the whole team right into the end-zone! Touchdown! We have ourselves a wedding!

Everybody's dancing... it's absolute bedlam. But what's this? It looks like a victorious Kitty is handing the power ball back to Bob and Paul. No, wait... that's not the ball... it's the bill.

· *Hers* ·

THE PRENUP

WHILE Donald Trump's divorce lawyer used to draw up six prenuptial agreements a year, now he's says he's doing six each month. Few of us have Trump-like assets to contend with, but the demand for prenuptial agreements is indisputably on the rise in middle-class America—even among young couples embarking on a first marriage.

This country's 50 percent divorce rate has become a largely accepted fact of life, and so these days, engaged couples and their families tend to approach weddings with more pragmatism and anxiety than ever before. While it's often the parents, not the bride and groom, who initiate the prenup as a way of protecting inherited property, trust funds, and interests in family businesses, sometimes couples who are absolutely passionately in love recognize that they need to properly address issues surrounding money before they enter into matrimony.

The problem is, negotiating a prenup is almost like negotiating a divorce before it happens. And who wants to be doing that while planning a celebration of a lifelong marital commitment? Corine went through a three-month prenuptial negotiation; even though she was willing to sign something to protect her fiancé's inheritance, his family wanted to tie up his current assets from year one to year fifty of their marriage. The negotiation boiled down to a fight between Corine's attorney and her in-laws' lawyer, and Corine and her fiancé found it hard to live with each other without taking sides. The good news is, Corine says, because she and her husband essentially went through a trial-divorce, they now have an even stronger relationship.

Even though women are increasingly coming to the marriage table with their own assets worth protecting, it's rare that both partners are equally in favor of the prenup. Often one person goes along with it because he or she just really wants to get married. The less powerful person ends up feeling she was coerced and that the marriage was conditional. The underlying resentment and mistrust may never get completely resolved: One woman told me that she and her husband fought so hard over the prenup and became so angry that their sex life suffered and it never really recovered.

Sometimes people try to cover all kinds of dictates in their prenups, from custody of future children to how often they should have sex to who does the laundry when. One husband-to-be tried to stipulate in a prenup that his wife's weight would not increase by more than twenty pounds over what it was on their wedding day. Obviously, there are limits to what is reasonable, and if you find yourself hashing out these limits during your engagement, it can seriously impact the wedding itself. Corine couldn't send out wedding invitations until her prenup was signed, and so for the three months it took to reach an agreement, she was left wondering if the wedding was going to take place at all.

In really difficult situations, sometimes the prenup is abandoned and the marriage goes forward anyway. Other times the marriage itself is abandoned. There were times when Corine had to force herself to remember that her fiancé was getting enormous pressure from his side, and that the financial details had nothing to do with the integrity of their relationship. There's no way around it; the prenup is one of the hardest things a couple can go through. It can truly be an acid test for the success of a marriage, and the key to survival is to go through it together, not as opponents but as a team.

· *His* ·

THE PRENUP

Aʜ, the wonders of the wedding season. The glorious ringing of church bells, the joyful tears of brides, the gleeful drooling of lawyers as they draw up their bills for prenuptial agreements. For those of you unfamiliar with the term, a prenup is a contract, signed by the bride, groom, their families, and their families' lawyers, that spells out who gets what in the event of a divorce. This contract, which may cost anywhere from $2,500 to $10,000 in legal fees, is typically put in place to protect an inheritance or assets that were earned previous to the marriage. Shared assets are often included. In fact, a prenup may be a complete divorce settlement in advance, with every eventuality negotiated, from future purchases of furniture, cars, and property to possession of pets and season tickets to the Yankees.

There are two sides of the prenuptial agreement fence. On one side, you'll find those who think it's hypocritical to have a signed prenup in your back pocket as you stand at the altar promising to eternally love, honor, and cherish your spouse. If you feel this way, it probably means you've invested some thought into the importance of the marriage you're about to create. It may also mean you're a romantic at heart: someone who believes a wedding shouldn't be about paperwork and protection of assets, but about real love—both the passionate kind you and your fiancée are sharing now and the comfortable, mellow kind you'll settle into after forty years of marriage.

What if your or your fiancée's family insists on a signed contract, and you disagree? Well, then you have to examine how important their assets are to you in relation to your marriage. Can you afford to sacrifice your inheritance for the sake of a contract-free marriage? Do you want to do so?

Then there are those on the other side of the fence, who believe it's wrong to romantically idealize marriage. These people look at the divorce rate in this country and understand that, for whatever reason, a large number of marriages simply don't survive. If you or your parents do want a prenuptial agreement, that's not inherently evil, it's just the facts of life. Just be sure your reasons for wanting the agreement are good ones. Trying to keep Daddy's money away from your wife's grubby, shoe-buying paws doesn't qualify as a particularly good motive. From the moment you say "I do," everything that's yours becomes your wife's as well. If this idea doesn't sit well with you, there's still time to call the whole thing off.

If you plan to work hard for the survival of your marriage through good times and bad, but you want disaster insurance for when all else fails, then you should feel confident approaching your fiancée about signing a contract. Odd as it may seem, there's no reason signing a prenuptial agreement can't be a somewhat romantic act. I'm not suggesting you do it while sharing a champagne bubble bath (the notary public may feel a bit out of place), but you can follow the signing with a candlelight dinner or a weekend getaway. Or you can accompany it with an equally binding contract of love—a promise to search each others' hearts, travel to every corner of the world and visit as many therapists' offices as it takes to find the secret of everlasting happiness together.

Most important, be sure to both emotionally and physically remove the legality of the prenup from the wedding ceremony itself. There is a priest who tells of arriving at a wedding rehearsal and learning that the prenup was still unsigned. The next day, the bride showed up for the prewedding photographs accompanied by her lawyer. The final negotiations were carried out in the back of the limo with the priest as a witness and the groom's attorney patched in via cell phone. Twenty minutes later, party one and party two were pronounced husband and wife. No tears of joy were shed.

· *Hers* ·

GIFT REGISTRY

WHEN little kids shop for a gift to give to adults, they'll probably pick out the latest Transformer for their father's birthday and the most rhinestone-encrusted pair of drugstore earrings for their mother. We humans are born with a tendency to purchase for others the very things we want the most. Some of us grow out of it; others grow up to be like Homer Simpson, whose great idea for Marge's birthday present was a bowling ball personalized with the name "Homer."

The gift registry is an engaged couple's magic shield against human nature. This isn't to say you shouldn't be grateful for anything anyone chooses to give you; a gift is a gift, and it's always the thought that counts. But you have to face the fact that when people shop and find something they'd love to see on their own shelf, they tend to buy it for you. From your engagement on, you'll be deluged with many such well-intentioned presents. Madeline's wedding guests all had bowls on the brain. She received more bowls than she could count, including one that was two feet in diameter. Someday she may come to appreciate them all, but in the meantime, she sure could use a salad spinner and maybe some forks.

Unless you want to end up like Jennifer, who received from the same person a vase for an engagement present, a vase for a shower gift, and a third vase for a wedding present, it's a good idea to register early and wisely. Make it as easy as possible for people to buy you a gift from the registry—in fact, make it easier for them to buy from the registry than to shop for an impulse gift. Many stores offer a toll-free phone number, and if you hook up with a few of them right away—preferably stores that aren't limited to just one state or one part of the country—then the instant your wedding gift becomes a gleam in someone's eye, he or she can punch a few buttons on the phone, and come up with the gravy boat of your dreams.

The experience of registering for gifts is singularly annoying. You go to stores or sections of stores you'd never ordinarily frequent, spending hours in Crate & Barrel or the housewares floor of your local department store. You drag your fiancé along, kicking and screaming, because these are his gifts too, and, like it or not, he should have a say in what the two of you ask for. He whimpers as you ask him to choose between china patterns; he moans as you ask his opinion on silverware; he whines as you ask him to decide which brand of bath towel will feel more comfortable on his fanny.

This is true of most, but not all, husbands-to-be. For Jeremy, the gift registry reflected the difference between how he and his fiancée felt about bigger relationship and lifestyle issues. Jeremy wanted to register for formal china and real sterling silverware, but his fiancée felt they should ask for items they could use right away. Jeremy believed his wedding was the time to receive things of lasting sentimental value, but his bride-to-be thought that, by the time they were ready to throw a formal dinner party for twelve, they would be able to afford to purchase fine silver and dinnerware for themselves.

The point is, registering for gifts is more complicated than you may think. It takes some serious time and a number of trips back to look at the same merchandise. And people will invariably complain that you registered at the wrong stores or too many stores or too few; that you registered for gifts that were too cheap or too expensive.

One solution that may please some of the people some of the time is to register on-line with sites like weddingchannel.com, theknot.com, and wedding411.com. Guests who feel comfortable shopping on the Internet will thank you for giving them a way to browse, buy, and ship your wedding gift while sitting around in their underwear. And those who don't will, in a perfect world, send cash.

But don't count on it. Despite the effort you put into your gift registry, you will receive plenty of unasked-for presents. Some people don't like ordering from computers or catalogs, particularly for a wedding, because they feel it's too impersonal. They like to see, touch, and smell the item they're giving on such a special occasion. Others just don't appreciate being told what to spend their money on as a gift, so they'll get you something they feel has a lot of personal value. Sometimes this works out for the best: Dave and I recently found ourselves serving toast to guests accompanied by the sterling silver jelly boat we never thought we'd use.

SEVEN SURVIVAL TIPS FOR THE GIFT REGISTRY (HERS)

1. Register for everyday flatware and dishes. You won't want to use the pricey stuff for casual entertaining.
2. Before you register for fine silver, think of your guest list. If only a few of the people you invited can afford it, you may get just one or two place settings. It can be a long time before you're in a financial position to complete the set yourself.
3. Don't register for vases or candlestick holders. You'll get lots of them anyway.
4. When picking china patterns, keep in mind that you'll be eating off these dishes every day for a long time. What looks cool today may look awful tomorrow. Go back and look at patterns several times on days when you're in different moods.
5. Cover a range of prices. Keep 20 percent of your gift requests below $75, 65 percent in the $100 range, and 15 percent over $150.
6. Register for luggage if you don't already have a good set. You'll need it for your honeymoon, and this is the perfect opportunity to replace ratty old dufflebags with nice suitcases.
7. It seems like everyone you know registered for one, but think long and hard before you put a Cuisinart on your list. They're a pain in the patoot to clean.

· *His* ·

GIFT REGISTRY

On the surface, registering for gifts sounds like a terrific idea. You get to go to any store you like, create a list of all the stuff you want, then give that list to everyone you know so they can fill your cupboards, closets, entertainment center, and garage with stuff you can't afford to buy yourself.

In reality, though, gift registry involves going to department stores you hate, picking out china and glassware you never knew you needed, compiling a list with no end after many weeks, and, when all is said and done, still being given fifty sterling silver picture frames.

Your fiancée and possibly her mother will drag you to Macy's, ask you to point to a china pattern you like, and laugh uncontrollably at your choice. Then they'll send you to the electronics department, where you will be allowed to register for one high-tech item (which no one will buy you).

Why you were invited in the first place remains a matter of debate. Maybe your fiancée wanted to pit you against the snotty bridal registry lady who has no time for anyone not named Jackie, Coco, or Ivana. If you need the registry lady's advice, after all, in her mind you're automatically too uncouth to understand it, and if you're not loading up on place settings for twelve, perhaps you'll find what you're looking for at your local K mart. Now, if you don't mind, she's running late for her eyebrow wax. Take this checklist, fill it out, and hand it to the clerk. And have a nice day.

Once you've made all your lists, you'll have to rely on your guests to learn for themselves where you've registered. There is no polite way to offer this information before they ask you for it. Including it with your invitation is obnoxious, and sending a separate registry notice is presumptuous. You just have to trust that those who don't call to inquire where you're registered will find out on their own, or give you cash.

Speaking of cash gifts, the common rule of thumb seems to be, "Give what you have." But if you're looking for real numbers, wedding etiquette experts say the appropriate range for cash gifts guests should give is $75–$100 for a single guest, and $100–$150 for couples. I'm giving you this information not so you can call your best man a cheapskate when he only gives you twenty-five bucks, but so you can properly gauge your reaction when you receive a truly generous cash gift. If some guests give you far more than you'd expect, or even far more

SEVEN SURVIVAL TIPS FOR THE GIFT REGISTRY (HIS)

1. Ask if you can be in charge of picking the highball glasses, which are the only crystalware you really give a hoot about.

2. You don't need $90 ice tongs. Besides, if someone gets them for you, you'll have to purchase the complementary $200 ice bucket on your own.

3. Put a really nice set of knives on your registry, along with a butcher block to store them in. For some reason, male guests love to give cutlery.

4. Register for a nice camera, so your honeymoon pictures will elicit lots of ooohs and aaaahs.

5. This is your chance to get some serious name-brand power tools. You may not receive them as gifts, but they're sure fun to look at while you're making your list.

6. Register for something really unusual. Your quirkier friends might prefer to give you the ten-gallon Super Soaker instead of a sugar and creamer set.

7. Pick a charity and give your guests the option of giving a donation to the needy in place of a wedding gift to you.

than you think they can afford, they deserve a special thank-you note, a thank-you phone call, and nice gifts in return when you attend their special occasions. What they don't want is for you to tell them that their gift was too much, so don't insult them by trying to give or send it back to them. Accept this gift and all gifts graciously, as they are all intended as symbols of friendship and love.

· *Hers* ·

VOWS

JUST as people may have a preference for sweet or salty foods, chocolate or vanilla, roller coasters or merry-go-rounds, there are definitely separate personality camps when it comes to choosing the vows that cement a marriage. Many people can't imagine having someone else put words into their mouths, and dislike the idea of merely repeating a conventional declaration of love and commitment. When these folks get married, there's no question that they'll write their own vows to reflect their personal meaning of marriage.

Others, however, prefer the formality of time-honored traditional vows. For people with strong religious beliefs, the rituals of their particular faith's matrimonial ceremony are what give weight and meaning to the nuptial bond. Whether for religious or personal reasons, some folks just can't imagine being married using "made-up" words. One celebrity bride was quoted as saying, "I didn't want to look back when I'm fifty and realize I'd said, 'You're really neat.' I'd rather stick to the classics."

In addition to the Traditionalist/Individualist line in the sand regarding wedding vows, there's also the Introvert/Exhibitionist conflict. Planning the wedding ceremony may fill you with anxiety if you're the kind of person who shudders at the thought of standing up in front of a room full of people (even your nearest and dearest) and publicly reciting your most intimate and personal feelings about your fiancé. He, on the other hand, was a theater major in college who can't wait to tell the world just exactly how he feels about you.

These personality differences may be one reason why you and your fiancé complement each other as a couple, but they can make it difficult for you to agree on your wedding vows. The last thing you want is to start off your marriage by mouthing words either of you is uncomfortable with. So here are some ways to find a compromise you can both believe in.

- Write your vows together. While some couples find it meaningful to hear their partner's personal pledge for the first time right there at the altar, the idea of writing down your deepest feelings, starting from scratch, can be terrifying. Working together is both reassuring and creatively stimulating.

- Compile the best of vows from various sources in a way that's meaningful to the two of you. You can also add personal touches to those existing traditional vows.

- Agree to be married using traditional vows, and arrange a moment during the ceremony or reception when you or your fiancé can express personal feelings in a reading, speech, or toast.

- Find a tradition that suits you both. If you are both drawn to the structure of traditional vows but are from different religious backgrounds, there are many nondenominational and pandenominational churches through which you can find vows that are both structured and universally meaningful. With a little research you'll be able to find existing vows that couldn't have been more perfect if you had written them yourselves.

· His ·

VOWS

MOST guys come from the "You tell me what to say and I'll say it" school of wedding vow preparation—the "you" being the officiating priest, rabbi, or justice of the peace. But then, most guys believe there are correct wedding vows that have been made official somehow, written by ancient scholars, adapted to each religious sect, verified by the Supreme Court, and signed into law by Thomas Jefferson.

Your religious institution probably does have standard vows that are recommended to couples who marry within their walls, but it's important to know that these are not set in stone. During your first meeting with your officiant, ask for copies of his or her suggested vows and review them on the spot, one sentence at a time, with red pen in hand.

While traditional vows never fail to bring tears to the eyes of wedding guests, they sometimes contain words or phrases that no longer make sense. Most modern brides would rather love, honor, and *cherish* their husbands than love, honor, and obey. Standard vows may also contain religious statements that don't mesh with your particular interpretation of your faith. Ask your officiant if you can change these passages without incurring the wrath of God, and if not, well, maybe you need a new officiant. Hint: it's better to find this out early in the process than on the day before the wedding.

If it hasn't happened already, one day during the planning of your wedding, your fiancée will approach you and say, "Honey, why don't we write our own vows?" The first thought that pops into your head will be something along the lines of, "Sure, honey, I'll just take a week off from work, put our search for the caterer and band on hold, ignore the work of ancient scholars and Thomas Jefferson, and write a five thousand-word treatise on the true definition of undying love with my little pad and pencil here." However, what you'll probably end up saying is, "Um, do you really want to?"

If she insists, it's not the end of the world. Many original vows are just slight variations on traditional ones with some personal thoughts thrown in. And the best vows aren't long at all, maybe two minutes of speaking time between the two of you, so you don't have to quit your job to become a writer. The best vows I've ever heard at a wedding took just fifteen seconds to recite. *Man:* "Do you take me for all that I am, and anything I will ever be, forever and ever?" *Woman:* "I do." And vice versa.

When you think about it, wedding vows are representations of your and your fiancée's personal beliefs about marriage, so the illogical approach would be to read something someone else has written. It's your life, your wedding, and your vow, so why not write something that has special meaning to you and your gathered family and friends? You're far more likely to remember and cherish your own words than those championed by some guy in a powdered wig.

· Hers ·

THE BACHELOR PARTY

IF you really want to know what might go on during your fiancé's bachelor party, you can read Dave's half of this chapter. But I wouldn't recommend it. This book is all about *surviving* your wedding and I'm here to tell you, the key to surviving the bachelor party is ignorance. The less you know about the bachelor party, the happier you'll be. You can't pitch a fit at your husband-to-be, who got so drunk he wet himself, if you don't know he did it.

In the domain of the bachelor party, the slightest interference by even the most tolerant bride in the world may get her pegged as a ball-and-chain-wielding tyrant. Therefore, you can't really have any say in what your fiancé does and doesn't do on his bachelor party night. But you can try to control some of the damage. Sit down early, when you begin to hear of a plan surfacing among his friends, and set the following ground rules for them and for yourself.

1. *If you live together, your fiancé must sleep somewhere else the night of his bachelor party.* Either that or you can arrange to stay overnight with a

friend or your parents. The last thing you want to do is wait up for him at home, glancing at the clock every five minutes as three A.M. comes and goes with no sign of the boys. To spare yourself the unpleasant sight of your beloved when he's drunker than a tick on a wino, simply remove yourself physically from the situation.

2. *You are not his emergency backup.* Has he forgotten the directions to the bar? Oh well. He shouldn't even *think* about calling you for help. If the boys get a flat tire on the road, the last person they should ask for rescue is you.

3. *You are not his hangover nurse.* The "in sickness and in health" deal doesn't go into effect until your wedding day. You don't deserve to watch him mope around in misery the day after his bachelor party; nor will you take care of his vomit. Suggest to your fiancé that he prepare in advance an emergency kit containing aspirin, bottled water, bread, a warm blanket, a bucket, and the remote control. After his bachelor party, he should hole up in a "hangover hut" (the TV room) and emerge only when he is a functional human being again.

4. *All signs of the debacle must be removed by noon the following day.* No admission stubs from strip clubs lying around; no panties in the sofa cushions; no sticky residue on the bathroom floor; no cigarette butts, beer bottles, or bodies.

5. *No lasting damage should be done.* Tattoos and any kind of body piercing are out. So, it should go without saying, are sexual encounters of any kind.

The bachelor party originated because it was once thought that grooms-to-be needed to get philandering out of their systems before their wedding day. Card playing or gambling was often part of the evening, with the winnings going to the groom so that he could afford another night out with the boys once his wife took control of the money. In our more enlightened times, the bachelor party has become an opportunity for your husband to get together with a lot of his friends who probably don't get to see each other as much as they'd like. Bachelor parties often are as harmless as a camping trip, a round of golf, or a ball game.

What's more common these days, in fact, is the increasingly debauched bachelorette party. People seem to think equality of the sexes means women, too, are dying for one last single-girl blowout. Usually this ends up as a night on the town doing all kinds of things you never really wanted to do when you were single: hanging out the windows of a limo screaming, or doing kamikaze shots with a male stripper named Thunder Down Under gyrating in your face.

Going out with the girls is a great way to have fun while the guys are out doing their thing, but wilder doesn't necessarily mean better, and you certainly shouldn't do it for revenge. Get all your friends together in one place and have fun the way you used to,

SEVEN SURVIVAL TIPS FOR TAKING THE FUN OUT OF YOUR FIANCÉ'S BACHELOR PARTY

1. Tell him one of the girls jumping out of the giant cake will be you.
2. Tell him one of the girls jumping out of the giant cake will be a man.
3. Tell him not to worry about you. You'll just be having a quiet drink with the male model who lives next door.
4. Plan a formal brunch with his parents the next day at noon.
5. Two hours before the party, mention that you think you might be pregnant.
6. Repeatedly whisper "You will not be an idiot at your bachelor party" into his ear while he's sleeping.
7. Introduce him to the perfect hangover cure: an early morning jog.

before the days of engagements and adult responsibilities. Have a great dinner out after spending the day doing something exhilarating, like mountain biking or rock climbing—or just unabashedly girly, like getting pedicures or going shopping. Spend a weekend with your best friends at a spa or go skiing. At least you'll remember that you had a good time, unlike old ice-pack-on-the-head over there on the couch.

· His ·

THE BACHELOR PARTY

YOUR bachelor party is your last chance to celebrate the freedom and perks you've enjoyed as a single man. Paying surgically altered women to take off their clothes, for instance. Or drinking until you are legally blind. While these activities may not be on your current list of "things I must do every Saturday night," they definitely won't be on your agenda after you're married. So, to quote from one of Tom Hanks' finer cinematic efforts, *Bachelor Party,* now is the time for "chicks and guns and firetrucks and hookers and drugs and booze!"

The responsibility for the no-holds-barred sleaze-fest known as your bachelor party traditionally falls upon the shoulders of your best man. It's his duty to call all your friends and male relatives, get them to agree on a place, date, and time, arrange for the food, drinks, and, ah... entertainment, and make sure you arrive without a clue about what's going to happen to you. Keep in mind, that puts a lot of pressure on one person. If your best man is your younger brother (under twenty-one) or a particularly shy individual, you may want to help him out by appointing a party committee made up of older, more outgoing friends.

It's okay to get involved in the beginning stages of planning your own bachelor party. That way, you can put capable people in charge, tell them what you want (maybe a baseball game) and what you hate (no farm animals), and give them a list of who to invite. Then let them go to it.

So what exactly can you expect? Count on having all the basic elements — booze, babes, hangovers. Beyond that, your bachelor party probably will fall under one of several time-tested themes:

The Lose-Your-Lunch Bowl. The group attends a baseball, football, basketball or hockey game. Offensive remarks are yelled at the players, much alcohol is consumed, and one member of the party is ejected for mooning the ump or ref. Dinner: hot dogs and warm Bud Lights. Follow-up: a sports bar, then a strip club, unless an all-in-one sports/strip establishment can be found. Cost for everyone but you: $75.

The Stay-Put Spectacular. Someone rents a boat or a house in the middle of nowhere, complete with a bar, a keg, two strippers, and their three-hundred-pound chaperone, Tiny. Drinking games are played, lewd acts are witnessed, and all car keys are locked in a kitchen drawer. Dinner: Domino's pizza. Follow-up: everyone passes out and wakes up with shag carpet imprints on their faces. Cost: $50.

Shots-R-Us. The gang commandeers a private room at a local bar or restaurant and drains the establishment's reserves of Sambuca and Southern Comfort, twenty shots at a time. Complaints from other patrons are filed, giant holes in the wall are created, and the night janitor quits after he sees what you did to the bathroom. Dinner: all-you-can-eat pasta. Follow-up: a really classy strip club. Cost: $100.

Hooker Heaven. Sometimes the hired women will do more than strip. Will they do it in a house? Will they do it if they're soused? Will they do it with your brother? Will they do it with each other? Back bedrooms are occupied, normal men are transformed into idiots, and you, being a classy guy, leave the debauchery to your unattached friends. Dinner: whipped cream. Follow-up: blood tests all around. Cost: $50–$200 (depending upon level of participation).

The High Roller. Everybody piles into a van and roadtrips to the nearest gambling attraction, whether it's a racetrack, riverboat, Native American reservation, Atlantic City, or Las Vegas. Cigars are smoked, free drinks are served, and much money is essentially flushed down the toilet. Dinner: comped hot plates at the all-you-can-eat buffet. Follow-up: presentation of the "Night's Biggest Loser" award. Cost: $300 minimum.

The Fake Kidnapping. Twenty ski-masked guys burst into your apartment or office, blindfold you, and stuff you in a car—or, in the case of wealthy friends, on a plane. You are taken to a strip club/bar/casino/abandoned warehouse, unmasked, and forced to wear a sign that says, "Buy me a drink, it's my bachelor party!" Dinner: bread and water. Follow-up: police and FBI inquiries. Cost: $100 or one night in jail.

The "Oh, Yeah, a Bachelor Party." Those grooms who put their trust in organizationally challenged party planners may end up with a night-before-the-wedding pseudo-party in the hotel bar. Rounds of gin and tonics are bought, girlfriends and wives drift in and out, and the highlight is Sports-Center on the bar TV. Dinner: usually the rehearsal dinner; if not, bar peanuts and Chex mix. Follow-up: two hours of sleep, four aspirin, and one ticked-off bride. Cost: $30.

Enjoy these graphic summaries now, because when your bachelor party is over, you probably won't remember a thing about it. One valuable tip: as the evening begins, ask your most responsible friend to keep you from doing anything stupid like driving or stumbling out into traffic—and to stop everyone else from pouring drinks into you when you've had more than enough. Your bachelor party may be the last chance you have to get totally out of control, but your really good friends will help you have fun with no damage more lasting than a hangover.

· *Hers* ·

THE BRIDAL SHOWER

THERE'S something about a wedding that has the power to catapult even the most self-determined, intelligent, independent woman right back into Barbie-doll girlhood. We may wear Manolo Blahnik stilettos under that white dress, but a white dress it is, and probably loaded with lace. Similarly, your bridal shower can bring you right back to the last time you got a whole bunch of girls together in one room to eat junk food, open presents, and talk about boys. Yep, that's right. Your tenth birthday slumber party.

Both your shower and a slumber party are marked by strange atavistic rituals—games of truth or dare and playing with the Ouija board turns into being crowned by a hat made of ribbons from your shower gifts. And it's almost inevitable that at some point in a bridal shower, a *Playgirl* magazine will surface. I still get chills remembering when my future mother-in-law handed me the centerfold in front of a videocamera and my husband's entire family.

There's nothing quite so strange as seeing a pack of grown women going into paroxysms of joy over trashy lingerie and kitchenware. Even if you couldn't have cared less about housewares before becoming engaged, you will after your bridal shower. Something chemical happens in your brain, and for a brief moment, you see yourself as a married woman actually using a rolling pin. (Thank goodness, along comes the bachelorette party to jolt you out of that nightmare.)

Making shower arrangements can bring out the worst in our dearest friends and closest relatives. One newlywed, Karen, told me that her relationship with her best friend was never the same after her wedding, because the friend initiated a battle with Karen's mom over who got to plan and host the shower. The friend felt it was her duty, as maid of honor, and the mom felt it was her duty, as, well, Mom. Eventually, the two joined forces and planned the event together, but no one was really happy with what had transpired—least of all Karen.

Let's not forget the brides who get a little greedy as they envision raking in all that stuff they registered for. Suddenly they think, "Wow, one more place setting and I'll be able to seat twelve for dinner!" They wonder aloud if any of their wealthier relatives coughed up for the Henkel knives. They drop little hints to the shower's organizers: "Remember, tell people the most important thing is to complete the silverware set!" I once went to a shower that lasted for six hours, the length of time it took the bride to open all her gifts. The invitation stipulated that guests were to bring a regular shower gift, a smaller "wishing well" gift, one or two boxes of cookies (the bride was a cookie fiend), plus a 10-by-12$\frac{1}{2}$-inch square of fabric "in the blue family" as a contribution to the bride's wedding quilt. Try not to be the kind of bride who allows her shower to be such a big deal.

It's important to remember that a shower doesn't need to follow set rules. If you don't like the all-girl thing, arrange a couples shower. If you don't want your shower to focus on the giving of pots, pans, and tap pants, suggest that it be just an occasion to get together and socialise, with no gifts.

There can be several showers for different groups of people in your life: a traditional shower for your mother and her friends who might expect it; a shower with your friends from your hometown; a co-ed get-together for all the people gathering for your wedding from out of town. Years ago, the point of a shower may have been to help the bride prepare her home, but nowadays it's really just another stage of the celebration. Look upon it as a time to get all your friends together in one room, eat junk food, open presents, and talk about boys.

· His ·

THE BRIDAL SHOWER

THERE'S one place you don't want to be, regarding your fiancee's bridal shower, and that's in the middle. In the middle is where a bunch of angry women yell at you. In the middle, you'll be forced into uncomfortable roles, such as facilitator, arbitrator, subservient pawn, exhausted listener, and scapegoat.

Most men are put in the middle when their fiancée's friends and female relatives have radically different visions for the shower; or worse yet, when they all disagree with what one of *your* female relatives wants. You step in because you don't want the problem to fall on the shoulders of your fiancée. Soon, you're begging your mother to apologize to her mother and negotiating a truce with her best friend.

Now, I don't mean to imply that men are the only reasonable gender. Plenty of guys have stopped talking to their best friends from kindergarten for no better reason than that they rooted for the wrong team at last year's Superbowl. I'm also not suggesting that every bridal shower turns into a catfight. In fact, the majority of these affairs are perfectly civil, flowing with the precision of a Swiss chronograph from the initial surprise to the serving of veggie dip to the presentation of scandalous lingerie.

But these are not the showers that strike fear into the hearts of men. My warning is aimed rather at the unfortunates who get sucked into a bridal shower maelstrom by the forces of evil and merciless fate. Those poor souls may have done nothing wrong in their lives aside from ignoring a few parking tickets or throwing rocks at the neighbor's cat.

Regardless of past transgressions, for the man caught in the middle, it's extremely difficult to escape. But not impossible. First, look around you for signs of sanity. Identify at least one calm woman and use her to help mollify the jerks, even if said jerk is related to you. Second, politely listen to the crossfire without taking a side. Quite often, the people involved just want their opinions to be heard. Third, offer alternatives—two separate showers perhaps, or one each for your fiancée's friends, her family, and your family. Fourth, ignore the enemy's threats. Words like "I'm not going to the wedding," "You can forget about getting a gift from me," and "Keep your nose out of it, buttface!" are often retracted as your wedding draws near. And finally, don't allow anyone to blame the problem on you. This is not your territory and, technically, not your fight, so there's no need get pummeled in the name of being a nice guy.

THE DING DING GAME

As long as there have been two sexes, people have been trying to figure out what men and women want from each other. Love, of course, as well as comfort, companionship, sex, and support. But in our day-to-day lives, all we really need is a couple of "Dings." Ding is the sound a member of one sex makes when his or her significant other does something pleasing. The nicer you are, the more Dings you get. A negative Ding means somebody screwed up.

To play the Ding Ding Game, the bride and the groom each need a small notebook. Every time one of you does something nice, the other assigns a predetermined number of Dings to the act and notes it in his or her diary. Keep this up throughout the prewedding period, then, on your honeymoon, take out your diaries and add up the Dings. Whoever has more gets footrubs every night of the trip. If you don't know how many Dings to give each kind act, here's a his and her guide to get you started:

The Bride

Tell the groom he doesn't have to register for china with you	+2 Dings
Tell him he has to take dance lessons	-2 Dings
Really expensive dance lessons	-5 Dings
Pick a wedding dress that shows off your cleavage	+6 Dings
Show him the vows you want him to read	0 Dings
Insist that he write his own vows	-4 Dings
Tell him he has to go to the bridal shower	-5 Dings
Tell him you have to go to the bachelor party	-10 Dings
Tell him you won't wait up for him after the bachelor party	+4 Dings
Wait up anyway	-5 Dings

Ask him to make the honeymoon arrangements	-1 Ding
You make the arrangements—to go to the Rum Punch capital of the world	+10 Dings

The Groom

Do what you're told and offer regular assistance	+4 Dings
Say "Yes, dear" a lot while channel surfing	-3 Dings
Dutifully follow your bride around while registering	+1 Ding
Praise her registry choices	+2 Dings
Suggest registering for a Sony Playstation	-1 Ding
Volunteer to write your own vows	+6 Dings
Assist in planning her bridal shower	+7 Dings
Attend your bachelor party	-1 Ding
Enjoy your bachelor party	-3 Dings
Fondle women at your bachelor party	-50 Dings
Tell your bride she's the only woman you'll ever love	+10 Dings
And that she could never, ever look fat	1 Big Ding-a-ling

The Event

·*Hers*·

THE REHEARSAL DINNER

At most rehearsal dinners, there's usually one old crone who pulls aside the bride's mother to whisper, "Now I know it's none of my business, dear, but just how long has your daughter been on these drugs?" You can't really blame her. After all, the bride is running around looking like a zombie, with dark circles under her red-rimmed eyes and ready to burst into tears at the slightest provocation.

At our rehearsal dinner, I basically hadn't eaten or slept in three days, and found it difficult to understand the simplest conversation. This fugue state can work to your advantage if you, too, have one of those families or circles of friends in which drama is likely to erupt at every moment. Sleep and/or food deprivation can serve as a natural tranquilizer.

Family skirmishes are fairly common at the rehearsal dinner. Your parents, for example, may be discovering at this point that you've decided to walk down the aisle alone. Perhaps they've lost the negotiation over the denomination of the church where you'll be married, and for the first time they're setting foot in the place where you'll be saying your pagan vows. Rehearsal dinners often bring together a roiling stew of divorced parents who haven't spoken in years, future in-laws and parents sizing each other up, your maid of honor and the groomsman who broke up with her last month, Democrats and Republicans, vegetarians and carnivores, Montagues and Capulets.

With all the mini dramas that are likely to ensue, it's easy to forget that the rehearsal dinner serves three primary purposes:

1. *Toast-making*. Toasts at the wedding are usually limited to the best man's speech, so the rehearsal dinner is when everyone else lets loose with humorous, more personal accolades. Of course, this can get out of hand. We went to one rehearsal dinner that turned into a revival tent, with people leaping up every sixty seconds to testify their love for the bride and groom. I think one woman fainted from the excitement.

2. *Gift-giving*. The rehearsal dinner is the perfect time to give gifts to the members of your wedding party. Unfortunately, since you're doing it in front of everyone, you have to make absolutely sure you haven't left anyone out. One bride forgot to bring the gift she'd bought for the flower girl, who in turn threatened to stall halfway down the aisle during the wedding. Another bride stirred a rebellion in the ranks of her attendants when they opened their gifts only to find hideous green earrings to match their hideous green dresses. "That wasn't a gift," one bridesmaid said afterward. "We were all hurt that the bride didn't give us something more personal."

3. *Last-minute-detailing*. You don't have to physically bring everyone to the place where you'll be married in order to rehearse the events to come. Many couples use the rehearsal dinner to go over details verbally, including transportation to the reception, arrival time at the ceremony site for attendants, seating procedures for ushers, and receiving-line instructions. One tip: Go over the highlights verbally, but make sure all the crucial details are down in writing. Prepare a written itinerary, and pass it out at the rehearsal dinner.

The rehearsal dinner is a chance to get all your favorite people together in one room for a party that's more intimate and less stressful than the wedding reception itself. Because there's less pressure on the rehearsal dinner being a "perfect" event (and because your in-laws are footing the bill), you can feel free to get creative and break some rules. It's traditional to host the rehearsal dinner for members of the wedding party, but there's no law that says you have to restrict the guest list to only those people. If guests are coming from out of town, it's a nice gesture to open the rehearsal dinner to everyone.

One last thing: there's no law saying the rehearsal dinner has to be a formal event in a restaurant. The dinners that people seem to talk about for years afterward are more casual and fun: a big backyard cookout, a harbor cruise, a pizza party. The less formal the event, the greater chance you'll snap out of your zombie state and enjoy what's going on around you.

· *His* ·

THE REHEARSAL DINNER

THE rehearsal dinner is supposed to be an evening of welcoming out-of-town guests, allowing the members of your wedding party to acquaint themselves, and making sure everyone knows exactly what to do during the ceremony. But it's really a chance for the groom's parents (who traditionally pay for and host the dinner) to try and upstage the bride's. In other words, it's the first round of a no-holds-barred personality clash/grudge match, pitting parent against parent, groomsman against bridesmaid, and often bride against groom.

In one common scenario, the parents of the bride pull into the valet parking area of the country club where the groom's parents are hosting the dinner, and immediately start to worry that the wedding they're financing will look, in comparison, like something the dog horked up on the kitchen floor. They enter the restaurant and are greeted by a tuxedoed maître d' who offers them a gift basket filled with expensive toiletries and curiously strong mints. "Why didn't we think of that?" the mother of the bride seethes, "and what on earth is that thing in the middle of the buffet table?!?" (It's a giant floral arrangement of a dollar sign). The bride's parents then consider one of two courses of action: taking out a second mortgage on their home to soup up the wedding in less than twenty-four hours; or hiring a hit man to take the groom's father's golden retriever for a really long walk.

In an opposite but equally interesting scenario, the parents of the bride pull into a dusty field where a hoedown appears to be taking place. The groom's parents wanted to give everyone a taste of how "partyin' is done is these hyar parts." Dinner is a whole pig roasting on a spit. The bride's parents consider pulling out their checkbook to ensure that every member of the groom's family has shoes to wear to the wedding.

Meanwhile, the bridesmaids are finding out which groomsmen they will be paired with as they walk down the aisle. Their choices are "hairy neck," "atrocious breath," "can't stop talking," and "greasy groper." From the groomsmen's point of view, they're privileged to escort "face like a stump," "larger than life," "no sense of humor," or "starting center for the Knicks." And everybody opens a wedding party gift except the two people whom you stupidly forgot.

The wedding rehearsal itself presents problems with which anyone who has ever assigned parts in a play will be familiar. Groomsman number two wanted to be the guy who rolls the runner down the aisle for the bride to walk on, and instead you told him to light some stupid candle. All groomsman number four gets to do is seat people, which he feels is a shameful underutilization of his talents. To prevent problems, you've asked the attendants on both sides to stand in order of height, which, of course, has created problems. No one wants to go where he or she is supposed to—clearly the bride's parents are going to stand wherever they want—and if your little brother asks one more "what if?" question, you've threatened to replace him with a chimp. You quiet everyone down the only way you can—by screaming at them to shut up and do what they're told. And on the fifteenth try, you run through the entire ceremony without interruption. The next day, at the wedding, the whole pack forgets it all.

In yet another, and frankly more common, scenario, the rehearsal is a lively, fun time for all, and the dinner is the very model of a gracious celebration. The groom's parents befriend the bride's parents (or strengthen their friendship), and the members of the wedding party mingle wonderfully, forming new friendships and reviving old ones. Gifts are exchanged and appreciated, and hilarious toasts are made by all.

Here's to a third scenario rehearsal dinner for you and your bride. May the bar tab be large and everyone's egos small. And may you end the evening with the warm, secure feeling that you are truly and deeply loved.

·Hers·

THE CEREMONY

As a result of built-up stress and anticipation, the last few days, hours, and minutes right before your wedding ceremony are prime bridal freakout territory. Warning signs include: a feeling of choking, hyperventilation, dry mouth, excessive perspiration, hot flashes, and brain freezes—complete with a look similar to that of a deer staring into oncoming headlights. Here are some ways to stave off ceremony panics:

Be prepared. Before or during the rehearsal dinner, go over the entire ceremony with your officiant and the wedding party. Review special assigned responsibilities: who stands next to each of you at the altar, who holds your bouquet, who arranges your train, who holds the bride's and groom's rings. Rehearse the roles of those assigned a special task—anyone who will light a candle, give a reading, or sing a solo. Make sure the ushers know who to seat when and where and can instantly identify your mother and your fiancé's mother.

Be firm. Now is not the time to make major changes or introduce new ideas. You were happy enough with your decisions a few days ago; there's no reason not to stick with them at the last minute.

Sleep. Sleep deprivation can make you do stupid things. If you're too wound up to sleep, going to the gym regularly will help you release anxious energy so you'll be able to get some rest.

Eat. You're not going to lose those last five pounds by starving yourself right before the ceremony.

Keep busy. Go to the movies, work on a latchhook rug, go shopping with friends. Do something productive with all your nervous energy: anything that will keep your mind off the wedding.

Pamper yourself. Get a manicure, a pedicure, a massage, and a facial.

If you take all these precautions, you should arrive at the twenty-four-hour countdown calm, smiling, and serene. Here's a handy guide to what you can expect from that point on.

24 HOURS BEFORE WEDDING (B.W.)
You try to eat, but are unable to keep down anything but bouillon, which turns out to be full of garlic. Panic. Brush teeth madly. Floss. Brush tongue. Run to drugstore and buy super-strength Listerine.

12 HOURS B.W.
Try to sleep. Pace. Awaken bridesmaid. Force bridesmaid to go to gym with you. After workout, note circles under your eyes. Cry.

3 HOURS B.W.
Discover you have actually gained a pound since the day before. Worry that dress won't fit. Discover that one shoe is missing. Arrive at wedding venue. Discover that the flowers look nothing like the ones you ordered. Realize you forgot to have wedding programs printed. Scream "Screw it!" (optional).

2 HOURS B.W.
Bridesmaids arrive to begin dressing. One has morning sickness and is run-

ning late. One is missing in action and feared A.W.O.L. Shoe reappears. Decide that your hair and makeup people completely screwed up and must start over from scratch.

I HOUR B.W.

Trembling hands force you to reapply mascara four times, since you're still not happy with the professional job. Still no bridesmaid, and photographer is irritated because he can't get pictures out of the way before ceremony.

45 MINUTES B.W.

Ushers arrive—all but one.

30 MINUTES B.W.

Having forgotten this isn't her wedding, your mother begins ordering people about. Organist starts the prelude. Ushers escort guests to their seats.

SEVEN SURVIVAL TIPS FOR ACHIEVING THE PERFECT WEDDING KISS

1. This kiss is too important to worry about smudging your makeup.
2. Know what happens to your breath when you haven't eaten in a while? Stash a Certs in your dress.
3. One kiss may not do it. Change head positions and give everyone a photo opportunity.
4. Think about the first time you two kissed. Imagine you're back there, alone.
5. No butt grabbing. This ain't the Playboy Channel.
6. Keep the tonsil hockey to a minimum. It's not Spin the Bottle either.
7. Look into his eyes. This is your first married moment together, and you'll want to remember it with your eyes wide open.

20 MINUTES B.W.

Groom and best man arrive. Missing bridesmaid and missing usher arrive together in state of disarray. Groom and officiant scuffle over who had the license last.

IO MINUTES B.W.

Standing in vestibule with your father, you are overwhelmed by emotion and realize 1) no one has a hankie and 2) your waterproof mascara... isn't.

5 Minutes b.w.

Groom's parents escorted to their seats. Hallucinate dancing cupcakes because you haven't eaten in five days.

1 Minute b.w.

Ushers lay the aisle runner. To save your life, you cannot remember your fiancé's name.

Ceremony Time

Minister takes his place, followed by groom and best man. Procession begins. Having gone catatonic, you enter a walking coma until awakened by the whoops and catcalls from the congregation signaling that you and your new husband are engaged in the longest public kiss in world history.

· *His* ·

THE CEREMONY

As the big day approaches, the average couple finds themselves buried under a suffocating mound of details. Wedding books provide minute-by-minute event timetables and in-depth checklists to ensure that you don't miss a single thing, but even if you and your fiancée slavishly check off each item, you're both still likely to miss something: your wedding. Oh, you'll be there all right, but without the proper state of mind, you may worry your way through one of your marriage's most important moments. Worse still, the pressure of planning everything, pleasing everyone, and paying attention to every little detail leaves many couples wishing that the whole mess was over and they were sitting on the beach in Tahiti.

Obviously, on the happiest day of his life the average groom would rather be happy—or ecstatic, or over-the-moon!—than nervous and impatient. And with the help of a few basic tips, hopefully we can get you there with bells on. To avoid checklist fever and make the most of your wedding ceremony, all you need to do is 1) Eliminate Unnecessary Worry (EUW!) and 2) Heighten Energy and Enjoyment (HEE!). Here are a few examples of each:

EUW! *Delegate, delegate, delegate.* Your job responsibilities at the ceremony should be limited to a) showing up and b) getting married. A week beforehand, parcel out time-consuming wedding-day tasks as follows. Paying the officiant and other hired help: the best man. Making sure everyone shows up on time: mother of the bride. Making sure guests sign your wedding book: one of the bridesmaids. Putting plants, place cards, and candles in their proper places: the groomsmen or ushers. Dealing with programs: ushers. Calming hysterical women: father of the groom and best man. Dealing with the throwing of rice, birdseed, confetti, popcorn, or cornflakes, the blowing of bubbles, the release of butterflies or the running of bulls: father of the bride. Miscellaneous crisis control: the biggest groomsman and the most reasonable bridesmaid.

HEE! *Prepare yourself physically and mentally.* If you hang out with friends and family the night before the wedding, talking, drinking, experiencing one last night of bachelorhood, make sure you leave the party early enough to grab five or six hours of sound sleep. Keep aspirin with you in case you wake up with a nervous (or shotglass-induced) headache. And allow yourself an hour or so in the morning to be alone with your thoughts. Take a long shower, and go through the steps of your ceremony and reception in your head. Then join your family and closest friends for a light breakfast. That should put you in the proper mood to get dressed and go to the ceremony smiling, calm, ready.

EUW! *If things go awry, let them.* Somebody important is bound to be late—it may even be you—and the schedule will inevitably be thrown off. News flash: your guests will wait! Calmly do what you have to do, and if important people don't show up, remain cheerful and improvise. Missing rings, ceremonial miscues, and uninvited guests are only a few of the monkey wrenches that may be thrown your way. These are not reasons to panic or stop the wedding, and you can always turn to your array of attendants and family members to take care of them for you.

HEE! *Be a gentleman.* Lavish attention upon your parents and those of your bride, and tell them how much you appreciate their help. Don't stand there like a lump at the altar while your bride is carrying around a busload of silk and sequins. Help her get around, give her your arm if you have to climb steps, assist her with the transport of the Loch Ness Wedding Dress if you both have to walk around the altar, and do everything you can to avoid stepping on any part of her clothing. One little rip and you'll get a swift kick out of the gentleman's club.

EUW! *Don't make last-minute changes.* Rest assured, you and your fiancée planned the wedding well. The decisions you made were the right ones, and no amount of screaming from maniacal parents or guests should sway you from your course. Twenty-four hours before the ceremony, you may hear protests: "What!!?? You're serving that cheap wine with dinner?" "You mean I have to sit next to my ex-wife?" "Oh, a DJ, how... ah... economical." You can listen to these voices of doubt if you want to, but changing things at the last minute only increases the chance of there being a problem, and in the end n-o-b-o-d-y e-l-s-e c-a-r-e-s.

HEE! *Act confident, even if you're scared out of your mind.* Go out and greet your guests at the door. Chatting with friends and people you haven't seen in a while will take your mind off your nerves, and limber up your tongue so you don't mess up during your vows. Speaking of vows, speak them loudly and say it like you mean it. Nobody wants to hear "I think maybe I do." Step up there, look your bride in the eye, and let her know she's the one. On this day, you're the man, the center of attention, the top dog, the one and only groom. To paraphrase the immortal words of the Beastie Boys, "You're the cheese and she's the macaroni."

Hers

READERS AND PERFORMERS

WHETHER your wedding is traditionally religious or secular, the participation of honored relatives or guests can make it a uniquely personal event. Adding a special reading or musical performance can ensure that your ceremony truly reflects the special relationship between you and your husband-to-be.

These days, people are personalizing both their ceremonies and their receptions. We've been to a wedding in which the groom's mother, a former opera singer, sang "Ave Maria" right before the vows; one where the bride's college writing professor read a poem he had written especially for the occasion; one in which the bride herself read a passage from Scripture; and one where the groom serenaded his bride down the aisle by uniting with his college woodwind quartet to perform the traditional processional march. During one reception, the bride's very musical family bumped the band offstage to perform an a cappella rendition of "You Really Got a Hold On Me." One of Dave's best friends brought tears to everyone's eyes by playing guitar and singing "You Look Wonderful Tonight" to his bride after their first dance.

Other creative ways to personalize a wedding? Get a tarot card reader or palm reader to circulate among the guests at the reception; organize a fireworks display for an outdoor wedding; give guests hand-held sparklers to hold as the bride and groom leave the reception; show a brief videotape or slides of special moments in the lives of the bride and groom; hire professional dancers for the reception to give a demonstration and group lesson in, for example, the swing or the rhumba.

Going above and beyond the typical Scripture/poem reading or hymn singing is a great idea—provided you bear in mind two things:

Keep it special. You're there to get married, not to provide a musical revue. There's no need to go overboard or get into some kind of competition to have the most unique wedding ever. Performance art or mimes or an appearance by your little sister's ballet troupe are not only unnecessary, they can also take away from the focus of the day—your wedding—and may not be understood or appreciated by your guests. The point of a reading or performance is to honor special friends in a way that reflects your and your husband's particular bond.

Keep it brief. One bride asked her best friend from college, who was unable to be a member of the wedding party, to perform a reading of her choice. Her friend decided to read the entire balcony scene from *Romeo and Juliet,* which—coupled with a rather long traditional Roman Catholic ceremony on a very warm summer day—elicited loud snores from an elderly relative who had nodded off. Remember, while your friend or godfather is up at the altar reading *War and Peace,* you'll be staggering under a cement truck of a dress, holding twenty pounds of flowers, and trying not to think about that itch on the bottom of your foot and the fact that your strapless bra has slipped down to your waist.

·*His*·

READERS AND PERFORMERS

READINGS serve two very important purposes at your wedding. One, they add spice and personality to your ceremony. And two, they provide a useful role for the spare family member whom neither you nor your fiancée could fit in your wedding party. Teenagers and doting aunts appear to be the most common readers at weddings, followed by thespian younger brothers.

When choosing people to read special passages from the Bible or a favorite poet, consider several factors. Readers should have reasonably loud speaking voices so that everyone gathered can hear. If you want your readers to speak into a microphone, have them practice using it beforehand so they can learn to avoid feedback and get accustomed to the echo of their own voice. They should be confident (and old) enough to perform in front of a big crowd. And they shouldn't have to read something you've forced upon them. Ask your readers to suggest passages that remind them of you, or have them write something original. Review their choices before the wedding, and agree on the ones you like best.

There are three places you won't find ceremony readings that win points for originality: in a wedding book, on a wedding Web site, and at other people's weddings. Try to go where no other groom has gone before. Check the poetry section of your local library—if you can't find something profound about love there, you must be stuck among the existentialists.

Regardless of the author or the reader, pretty much everyone appreciates an appropriate literary reading. But for some reason, most guests fancy themselves discerning critics the minute a musical performer steps up to the mike. Admittedly, we've all seen family "musicians" at weddings flailing on a cheap guitar with 100 percent passion and 0 percent skill or striving for the multiple colors of four-part harmony and ending up with the sonic equivalent of brown. My advice to you is, be careful who you ask to perform at your ceremony, and stay away from less traditional instrumentalists like the mouth harpist, flugelhorner, or one-man band. And after your chosen performers do their stuff, be sure to lavish compliments on them, even if they weren't as great as you expected them to be.

Finally, even if your reader is Kurt Vonnegut, your organist is Billy Joel, and your vocalist is Luciano Pavarotti, keep the number of ceremony performances to a minimum. A Wagner opera may have many acts, but the more you put in your wedding program, the more your guests will be praying for the fat lady to sing.

·*Hers*·

THE RECEPTION

TIME flies, it's said, when you're having fun. But that's nothing compared to what happens to time when you're getting married. As a guest at a wedding, you're aware of a leisurely progression from first dance to bouquet tossing to cake cutting. But as a bride, you're aware of nothing more than a haze of happy faces and helpful hands guiding you from place to place. Ten minutes after you've said "I do," it seems, you're sitting in the back of a limousine with your new husband, wondering where your wedding went.

Time gets sucked into a black hole at your wedding. You catch yourself at odd moments thinking, "Wait! Stop! I want to remember this!" Then you're being hoisted up onto a chair for the hora or having your garter removed in public, and you're thinking, "Wait! Stop! Why am I *doing* this?" People will tell you afterward about things that happened and show you pictures of scenes you'll have absolutely no recollection of.

Since time is controlling you at your wedding reception, rather than the other way around, there's only one way to make sure it's the event of a lifetime. Stop trying. That's right; let go. You've spent twelve months attempting to control everything and everyone around you, and now is the moment of truth when you must allow what you have created to proceed on its own momentum. There's nothing you can do, and nothing you *should* do, except relax and let people tell you how beautiful you look.

Straight from the mouths of dozens of recent brides, here's more advice for getting maximum enjoyment out of your reception:

Eat. You don't have to eat a lot, but put something in your stomach. You agonized over the selection of the food, you deserve to taste it. Besides, you don't want to pass out after having one glass of wine on an empty stomach.

Drink. You'll probably lose eight ounces of water for every five pounds of dress you carry around all night. Make sure you stay hydrated by drinking water, not just alcohol.

Don't worry about visiting every table. It would be nice if you got to see everyone at your wedding, but don't let the obligation to do so keep you from enjoying the people you're with at the moment. Guests who leave early will find their own way to offer their personal congratulations.

Spend time with your husband. If you must split up to go around to the various tables, make an effort to find each other periodically throughout the night. You want to experience your wedding as a couple, not as separate individuals who meet up only at the first dance and the cutting of the cake.

Resist being a crisis manager. You've handled so many problems during the planning of your wedding, it may be tough to resist the impulse to take over when the ten-year-old ring bearer, after sneaking his second beer, gets sick in the corner. There are people whose job it is to handle things like this.

Be yourself. Your wedding has been built up to be such a momentous occasion that you wonder if you shouldn't be talking about momentous things or behaving in a way other than you ordinarily would. It's tough to act like there's nothing unusual going on when you're dolled up in white tulle and a gallon of makeup, but remember that underneath you're the same person you always were, and the people you're speaking to are the same as they've always been.

Reach out. As the center of attention, you think you'd be besieged by people wanting to talk to you. But sometimes guests are reluctant to approach, respecting how in-demand the bride must be. If all your guests think you're too busy for them, you may start to feel isolated at your own wedding. Go out and approach the people you want to talk to.

Leave when you want to leave. Some couples stay at their reception until the last guest leaves and the band is packing up. Others want to make a grand exit at the peak of the festivities. Decide ahead of time with your fiancé which departure sounds better to the two of you so that leaving your wedding doesn't start a fight on the big day.

Have a postwedding party with friends. Movies show scenes in which the newlywed bride and groom bound down the stairs of the church—with guests straining for a last glimpse—and dash into a limo en route to the airport. But can you imagine flying to Mexico in a ball gown? Many couples spend their wedding night in a nice hotel and leave for their honeymoon the next day. Wouldn't you rather spend part of that night in comfortable clothes, in the hotel bar or at the home of a friend or family member, catching up with all the people you wished you'd had more time to talk to at the reception?

Smile. During her reception, one bride announced, "I'm so happy my cheeks hurt!"

· *His* ·

THE RECEPTION

THE kickoff to most wedding receptions is the formal receiving line, where the bride, groom, and their parents receive hearty congratulations for succeeding in pulling off a wedding. If you've ever worked in the fast food industry, you already know the script for dealing with a large number of people in a short amount of time. "Hello, welcome to our reception. May I take your warm wishes for our lifelong happiness, please? Would you like to give us an expensive gift with that? Your table is number 13 near the potted ficus; enjoy your free meal. Thank you for coming. Next, please."

Then it's on to the reception proper, either at a different location or at a different area of the ceremony site. Your guests partake of the cocktails and hors d'oeuvres you painstakingly selected, while you go hungry getting your picture taken eight thousand times. After one final shot of you, your new wife, and her distant cousins, you are whisked to the middle of the reception hall and announced as husband and wife for the first time. Then, in rapid order, comes the first dance, a blessing, a toast, a meal, more dancing, greeting each table, throwing the bouquet and garter, cutting the cake, the last dance, and whammo, you're off to Jamaica!

The day goes by so quickly, you may wonder how you could have spent a year planning it. But despite the fact that you'll barely eat, sit, or stop talking as you're being yanked from one place to the next at breakneck speed, your reception can leave you with a lifetime of wonderful memories. Not to mention a few moments you would rather forget. Okay, I'll mention them anyway.

You'll love to remember being the center of attention. You may never have had the experience of people lining up just to talk to you, or raising their champagne glasses to toast what a great guy you are. Especially if you grew up in a large family, you may never have been first to get anything. Now you're at the head table, first to get served, first to dance, and first topic on everyone's lips. Even grooms and brides without a selfish bone in their bodies can't deny the pleasure of being King and Queen for a Day. Enjoy the attention while you can, because only one thing will put you back into the spotlight after your wedding, and that's babies.

You would rather forget all the worrying you did. Many couples spend at least part of their reception asking themselves stupid questions. Is it going well? Why isn't anyone dancing now? Are they having a good time? Why don't they serve dinner already? Why is that music so loud? When it's all over, there will only be one question you wish you had asked: Who cares? Your guests will have a good time because they like you and they see you having a good time.

You'll love to remember the little things that go wrong. A strange fact of life is that we often remember the mistakes we've made more clearly than the successes we've had. After weddings, the effect is even more pronounced. Who wants to hear about how lovely your bride looked when they can recount how you tripped and fell on top of her during your first dance? I guarantee you and your friends will tell far more stories about what went wrong at your reception than you will about what went right. Sometimes imperfections are just more fun.

You would rather forget the fifty times you had to stop and kiss the bride because some clown started dinging his soup spoon against a water glass. The first time, it's cute. The second time, it's sweet. By the fifteenth ding, enough already. You start to feel like one of Pavlov's dogs, only instead of salivating in anticipation of food at the sound of the bell, you're steaming in anticipation of stuffing that spoon somewhere entirely uncivilized.

You'll love to remember the various people you've brought together in one place at a single moment in time. There's your delinquent friend who was banned from your house during high school, all dressed up in a tuxedo and dancing with your mother. There's your uncle Joe laughing with his current wife and all three of his exes. There's your two-year-old niece posing for pictures with your ninety-year-old grandmother. Few feelings compare with that of stepping back from your reception and seeing all the people you love.

· *Hers* ·

GUESTS

WEDDINGS, like office Christmas parties, are breeding grounds for uninhibited behavior. For many guests, your wedding marks the first opportunity they've had to get out since Cousin Ethel's funeral back in '42. For others, preoccupied with changing diapers and schlepping the soccer carpool, the last time they really partied was Woodstock. Meanwhile, younger guests tend to adhere to one standard of behavior whenever there's drinking and dancing, whether it be your wedding or the annual Kappa Sigma Barf & Blow fest. And the really small fry can have a hard time distinguishing between a holy water basin and a urinal.

Here's an overview of who you can expect to see at your wedding:

The Drunk. Where there's alcohol, there's fire. Someone at your wedding is going to drink too much and pick a fight, have an emotional breakdown, make a pass at the wrong person, have sex with the wrong person, do a Travolta imitation on the dance floor, spill a secret, start a feud, or put on a strip show. Be ready when it happens.

The Eager Beaver. See those flashbulbs popping? Yep—that's your godfather, who's so proud of you he could bust. In fact, he's so proud he's about an inch away from your face trying to get the perfect shot as you're trying to focus on other things, like repeating your vows. Tell him nicely that you're paying someone to do that, a professional who can get the same picture with a telephoto lens from the balcony.

The Thoughtless. How many weddings have you attended in which a peanut gallery sits right behind you, making editorial comments on everything from the bride's dress to the length of the ceremony to the estimated cost of the affair? Thoughtless guests talk incessantly. They smoke and dump the ashes in the floral arrangements. Their cell phones ring during the ceremony.

The Oblivious. A subset of the Thoughtless, but more forgivable. These folks will call you the day before the wedding and assume you have time to answer questions such as, "What time is the ceremony again? And can you give me directions? I've lost the ones you sent." Or "It says 'Black Tie' here. I'm just calling to find out what you think I should wear."

The No-show. One bride told me her boss canceled at the last minute, but instead of telling her he wasn't coming, he told another guest to pass the message on. After the bride returned from her honeymoon, her boss said, "Sorry I couldn't make it. I've already sent you a check." She and her boss aren't on very friendly terms anymore.

The Young. Babies cry. Children laugh, scream, stomp, and shout embarrassing things. If you have a lot of young 'uns at your wedding, you may experience all of the above.

What can you do? Well, the first trick is to divorce yourself from your guests' behavior. It's no reflection on you, and you can't let it spoil your good time. Anyway, you'll probably be so overwhelmed by what's happening to you that you won't be able to focus on what other people are doing. It's only afterward that you'll hear about the fire the flower girl started in the bathroom.

The most contact you will have with your guests is during the reception, when it's traditional for bride and groom to make a trip around the room and talk to those seated at each table. It's especially important for you to pay attention to those who have traveled to your wedding from far away, and have paid serious bucks to be there. Older guests and people you rarely see take priority over closer friends and family members.

The other opportunity for face time with your guests is the dreaded receiving line. Most guests hate going through receiving lines, and most brides and grooms hate standing in them. But any wedding with an attendance of more than fifty traditionally demands a receiving line, because it's one way to absolutely ensure that each and every guest gets to spend a bit of personal time with you. Assign to your parents or a trusted bridesmaid the task of tactfully keeping the line moving, and try to look on the bright side of having the chance to see so many loved ones all at once. If all else fails, have a drink beforehand, or remind yourself, to quote one new bride, "Whatever. I'm married."

·*His*·

GUESTS

SINCE most people have attended at least one wedding by the time they're ready to plan their own, the role of "wedding guest" is one you've probably had firsthand experience with. You've seen what a wedding is like through the eyes of someone who has little invested in it besides a gift-wrapped waffle iron. And you know that many wedding guests will—when left in their natural state—snore through the ceremony, scarf down dinner, and try to get home as early as possible. To shake off this natural inertia and make a wedding reception fun for the guests and a success for the bride and groom, each person present needs a good reason to get off his or her butt and shake it around the dance floor. Typical good reasons are:

1. Lots of fun friends are there

2. The band sounds just like Abba

3. The alcohol is free

While two and three are dictated by your budget, reason number one can be arranged with some thoughtful and creative guest list tinkering. This is a little process I like to call enhancing the Guest Quotient (or GQ) of your reception. In case you haven't heard of the GQ, it's one of the more reliable indicators in judging whether your wedding reception is a doozie or a dud. GQ is measured on a scale from 0 to 200, with 0 being a flop; 100 being average; and 200 is fun, fun, and more fun for all. Through a complex system of linear probability sequences and double-blind studies, scientists have arrived at the following definitive criteria for measuring the GQ of any reception:

GQ: 0–40. Nuptially braindead. Average age of guests: 65. Nobody's dancing, no one is mingling, everyone's yawning, and the disposable cameras on each table still have 23 exposures left. Warning sign: you catch one guest reading a book.

GQ: 41–80. Matrimonially disabled. Average age: 45. The wedding singer is daring people to dance, a game of Pictionary just broke out in the corner, and the only thing the bartender runs out of is tea. Warning sign: someone asks you where you got the life-size wax figures seated at table 12.

GQ: 81–120. The marital median. Average age: 35. Old people leave early, young people hang out. There's dancing when disco is played, mild chatting and buffet nibbling the rest of the time. Warning sign: only two guests take off their suit jackets.

GQ: 121–160. Bridally brilliant. Average age: 25. The dance floor is rocking, strangers are exchanging phone numbers, Grandma is cutting a rug, and the bartender has to announce last call four times. Designated drivers and lost clothing are rampant. Warning sign: more than five male friends say, "I love you, man."

GQ: 161+. Something illicit, something wild, something illegal, something weird. Average age: apparently 2. Your best man's climbing the bell tower, table five is naked, your divorced friends are noisily making up in the ladies' room, and somebody brought a llama. The evening ends with a pile-on and a body count. Warning sign: Cousin Jack's eyeballs are bleeding.

Most couples shoot for a GQ in the 130 range—a memorable ceremony and reception that doesn't necessitate a visit from the cops. In order to achieve this high score, you have to mix the guest list and seating arrangements like a perfect pot of chili, adding just the right touches of mild and wild elements, then simmering to a slow and steady boil. This brings us to enhancing the GQ—something you can do in five easy steps:

1. Invite lots of "fun igniters," the kind who like to jump up and go "hey everybody, let's have a sock hop!"

2. Put one really fun person at every table.

3. Seat young and old folks together regardless of family ties and who knows who.

4. Appoint one groomsman and one bridesmaid as the party police. It's their job to get even the most curmudgeonly guests to do the Hustle.

5. Be the life of your own party. Don't look at visiting each guest as a chore, think of it as a game. Try to get each guest to smile. Dance with every child under four. Propose a toast, hand out cigars, make jokes, be merry. If you're having the time of your life, your guests will follow your lead.

· Hers ·

DANCING

At a certain point in the wedding planning, a man thinks he's made it over the hump. He's suffered through consultations with the caterer and count-less discussions about flowers and doilies. He's watched with feigned interest as you paraded dozens of bridesmaid dress patterns by him. He's registered for guest towels. And with the wedding not far off, he figures he's home free. This is the perfect time to bring up his most primal fear: dance lessons.

Your vision of the first dance at your wedding is a lot like Cinderella at the ball. The orchestra strikes the first chords of a lush waltz, your prince takes your hand and sweeps you onto the floor. He leads like a dream as you move around the room effortlessly in his arms, his eyes never leaving yours, until the final note, when he dips you way back and takes your breath away with the perfect kiss.

However, his view of the first dance is more like "Oh, God, please let it be over." Nothing could be worse than the trapped-in-a-fishbowl feeling he experiences on the dance floor. At the zillions of weddings we've attended in the last few years, only one groom admitted to looking forward to his first dance with his new wife. He happened to be the son of a professional dancer. The vast majority of men have deep-seated problems with any style of dancing that doesn't resemble a seizure.

So here's how to get your fiancé to spend a few hundred bucks for ballroom dancing lessons. First, ask him to picture in his mind the average female dance instructor. Ideally, this is as close as he will come for the rest of his life to a beautiful woman who isn't you. Second, tell him there will be other reticent husbands there and that he can commiserate with them between fox-trots. Third, explain to him how great it would be to make the first dance at your wedding truly special instead of just one more tradition to fret your way through. Describe how reassuring it will be to fall back on prepared and dutifully rehearsed steps when you're on display in front of your friends and family. As a last resort, tell him that, if he doesn't take lessons with you, your first dance will be with the best man. That should do the trick.

Once he agrees, be prepared for him to experience a painful learning curve. Not that you're going to pirouette around the studio on the first day either, but of the two of you, who is more likely to be able to follow a beat and remember steps? Probably the one with seven years of aerobics classes, five years of ballet lessons, a year of gymnastics or ice skating, and two years of cheerleading under her belt. In your husband's first few hours of ballroom dancing, he will have less than no clue what to do. He'll slowly puzzle out where his feet go next in the box step. Here's a hint—it's a square! You know how he makes fun of you whenever you try to play softball? "You throw like a girl!" he'll say, as if you were trying to be something other than female. Now's your chance to get back at him. "First day with the new legs?" is my personal favorite.

Eventually, with the help of a patient instructor, you'll both start to get a feel for the steps, and it will be time to arrange your first dance. Most couples go to their lessons having selected a song that was playing when they first met, or one that represents a particularly meaningful period in their relationship. Unfortunately, not every song is right for ballroom dancing. A lot of pop or rock songs have some kind of funky tempo change in the middle that turns a tango into a swing. Remember at your high school dance, when the band played "Stairway to Heaven" as the last song? Every couple was standing and swaying, and suddenly..."*And as we wind on down the road—Bam-ba-bam-ba-bam-ba-bambam-bam!*" Still clutching their dates, everyone tried to keep slow dancing—quickly. Clearly you don't want that to happen in the middle of your first dance. So try to stick with a song that's steady throughout, or go with a piece that was actually made for ballroom dancing.

Once you've got your song, find out what step it is. Waltz? Cha-cha? Tell the instructor you want to learn more than the basic moves. Throw in a few turns and spins, some minor variations on the theme, but don't get overambitious. Instructors will be happy to teach you the Whirling Dervish Double Dip, but chances are you'll completely forget it when the moment of truth rolls around.

Another thing about dance lessons. Most dancing schools are filled with couples who are preparing for their weddings. And most dancing schools like to make money, which means the instructors will try to keep you coming back after your wedding by telling you what great dancers you've become in such a short time. After a few lessons, you may be asked into the manager's office. He or she will evaluate your class performance (upper tenth percentile without a doubt), and convince you that it would be a disservice to humanity if you quit the dancing habit now. You may then be pressured into buying a year or more of dance lessons at gym membership–level prices.

You and your fiancé should discuss your reactions early in the dance lesson process. If you find you both love dancing, then by all means continue to pursue the hobby. But if you're just taking lessons to add a little fun to your wedding and to avoid embarrassing yourselves, it's perfectly all right to purchase only the bare-bones dance instruction package and end your ballroom career before it begins. Be prepared to tell that pushy manager to shuffle off to Buffalo.

· His ·

Dancing

MAYBE you're that one guy in ten who has rhythm. You've got the music in you. You love the nightlife. You actually have, in your closet, a pair of boogie shoes. If so, you should know that the rest of us hate you. You and all your John Travolta buddies have been stealing our dates for quite some time now.

If you're like me, you've avoided dancing ever since that excruciating moment in sixth grade when Jenny Johnston dragged you out to the middle of the gym floor in full view of all your friends. Sometimes, in a bad moment, you flash back to the smell of sweat socks and the sound of Human League echoing off the cinderblock walls. Your elbows are raised as you step to the right in a desperate attempt to locate the beat. Then comes the inevitable pointing and laughter.

At high school functions, the slow dances were always your saving grace. All you had to do was wait for the cover band to break out Journey's "Open Arms" and then *you* were in charge. Swaying from side to side, arms wrapped tight around your latest girlfriend-for-life, sweating like crazy but afraid to let

SEVEN SURVIVAL TIPS FOR DANCING AT YOUR WEDDING

1. Get out on the floor. The rest of the guests take their cues from you.
2. Everybody looks like a dork doing the Electric Slide. Do it anyway. It's fun!
3. Be gentlemanly. Both grandmothers, both mothers, all girls under ten, and the least obnoxious bridesmaids should get a dance with you.
4. Close your mouth. We don't want to see you counting steps.
5. The open collar and bow tie around the bare neck looks great on dancers at Chippendale's. It's not for you, Mr. Cheez-Lover's Pizza.
6. Put your drink down. Hold your wife's hand instead.
7. Dance with your bride—more than just the first and last dances. Get out there and show her why she married you.

go. As long as you had a suitable partner, nobody ever laughed at you for slow dancing.

Fast-forward to your wedding day, when you and your last-ever girl-friend-for-life will spend part of your first hour as an officially married couple dancing. Just the two of you. In full view of all your friends and family. Are you really going to fall back on the old clutch and sway?

Actually, yeah. Provided that's okay with your fiancée, and you pick an appropriately slow first-dance song. If you were any kind of a dancer, most of your guests would know it by now. As it is they don't expect anything more from you than a devoted gaze into your bride's eyes as the two of you move lovingly together in a modest circle. In other words, if you don't want to add dance lessons to an already hectic wedding preparation schedule, chances are good your loved ones won't know the difference.

That said, there will be at least one lively older couple at your wedding, usually someone's Aunt Selma and Uncle Charlie, who really know how to cut the rug. They'll waltz, tango, jitterbug and fox-trot their way through the crowd like Fred and Ginger, making you and your wife feel like Fred and Barney.

If this is the kind of thing that makes you envious, then a few dance lessons now can certainly help. Dance instruction schools are easy to find in the Yellow Pages, and if cost is an issue, tell your parents you want to learn ballroom dancing so you can look like adults at your wedding. Even the most penny-pinching folks will probably pay up.

One word of warning: Wendy and I went the dance lesson route, and for months we practiced and practiced the fox-trot that was to be our first dance. When our wedding day arrived, we were ready. The first notes of our song filled the reception hall, we completed one spin, heard some enthusiastic clapping and cheering, and then the dance floor filled with other couples. Within seconds, our lessons abandoned us, and we were mingling, laughing, and clutching and swaying for the remainder of the evening. Sounds like two hundred dollars worth of dance lessons down the drain, right? Not really. It was worth it just to hear those few seconds of applause.

THE RESPONSIBILITY
ASSIGNMENT QUIZ

The key to a successful wedding day is delegation of authority. So let's find out how good you are at leading the troops. Assign each situation, crisis, and responsibility in the left column to the appropriate person in the right column by drawing a line from one to the other. You don't want to overload anybody, but you want each problem to be handled correctly. The challenge is to assign each responsibility to a different person.

Transportation from ceremony to reception	The groom
Restaurant for rehearsal dinner lost the reservation	The bride
Bride faints at the altar	Father of the bride
The organ	Mother of the bride
Seating the right guests in the right place	Father of the groom
The wedding rings can't be found	Mother of the groom
Reader is too nervous to perform	The best man
Making sure the food is served on time	The maid of honor
Unwelcome guest shows up	The groomsmen
The groom is drunk	The bridesmaids
The music is too loud	The caterer
Bride and groom haven't greeted everyone yet	The officiant
Someone put his elbow into the cake	The DJ or band-leader
Mom won't stop crying	The consultant
Nobody's dancing	Your largest friend
It's time for everyone to leave	God

The Aftermath

....

· Hers ·

THANK-YOU NOTES

My husband has a selective memory when it comes to the details of our wedding. If you asked him whether he was involved in the planning, he would respond with deep indignation. "Of course I was! Not only did I pick the reception hall, I booked the DJ, found the minister, taught the organist how to play 'Here Comes the Bride' and then baked the cake all by myself."

Similarly, he seems to recall taking an active role in the writing of the thank-you notes. Now, whether or not you believe in this Men/Mars, Women/Venus thing, you have to admit that women have certain instincts that men lack. Have you ever heard of a married couple in which the husband does all the holiday gift shopping for both their families? Is the husband ever the one who remembers to send birthday and anniversary cards and baby gifts? Of course not. These small social niceties are dependent on a small microchip most women have, and most men, sadly, do not.

That mysterious social microchip is the only way to explain how we women somehow know in our guts that there is a ritual in which thank-you notes must be written for every wedding gift we receive and that we must begin planning for that ritual early.

Therefore, I'd be skeptical of any man who says, "Oh, yeah, the thank you notes. I wrote those." What he means is, yes, he brought his wife a pen and a glass of water as she sat down to write the notes and lick the envelopes. Perhaps he turned down the volume on the television in order to help her concentrate. He may have even looked up an address or two. But did he come up with the perfect phrasing to make his aunt Connie feel like a million bucks for her gift of a handmade sculpture of mating turtles? Did he keep diligent track of each gift that came in and each corresponding note that went out? Did he lie awake at night wondering if his great-grandmother is putting a stop on her check because she hasn't received acknowledgment within the expected month of its receipt? I think not.

Rather than setting yourself up with doomed expectations when it comes to thank-you note writing, I suggest you accept the fact that the burden of the writing will be on you. You can, however, assign your mate certain specific tasks that will otherwise lighten the load. Here is my suggested division of labor:

Your Job	Your Husband's Job
	open the gift
	put the gift away
	record the gift and giver in a special "gift log"
	bring you blank notecard and envelope
	bring you pen
	bring you cookies
write gracious note	*stamp and address envelope*
	mail note

Seriously, thank-you notes aren't really that tough a chore. I'm not saying writing them is a bucket of fun, especially if you had five hundred guests at your wedding. But if you write a note for each gift as it comes in, rather than procrastinating and being stuck with a whole mess of them to write belatedly, you'll find the process much less onerous. Writing one note a day is infinitely less annoying than writing thirty notes once a month. If your note is sent out promptly, your guests won't worry that their gifts got lost in the mail, and they will feel you truly appreciated their thought.

Do try to be gracious in your notes. You and your husband can snark all you want in private about Aunt Connie's sculpture, but you'll only regret it in the long run if you let your true feelings emerge in sly between-the-lines humor. Wedding gifts have become such an expected part of the wedding ritual that we often start to believe our guests owe us a gift from our registry, or that their attendance at the wedding is worth a certain amount of money. A sincere thank-you note is your chance to convey your appreciation to your guests for caring enough to help you celebrate your wedding day and giving you a little piece of themselves to help preserve the memories.

· *His* ·

THANK-YOU NOTES

FOR many men, the most troublesome part of this whole process isn't the wedding, it's the thanking. Ever since you were ten, when your mother made you write to your grandparents thanking them for the ridiculous Big Bird sweater you felt you were too old to wear, you've hated thank-you notes. "No," you were told firmly, "just saying 'thank you' when you get the gift is not good enough. Go write Grandma a nice letter right this instant!" First, you had to find a clean sheet of paper, then a decent felt-tip pen that hadn't dried up, and then you were faced with that dreaded blank page.

"Dear Grandma and Grandpa: Thank you so much for the terrific sweater. Gee, it is neat. I wear it sometimes. Thanks a lot." You knew it barely qualified as a piece of civilized correspondence, but you were so eager to get it over with, you filled the page with whatever came to mind. Then came the computer and the dawn of the instant, space-age thank-you note, which eliminated that drawer full of dried up felt-tip pens but gained you nothing in the personal, heartfelt sentiment department.

Now you're getting married and the gifts are going to come in fast and furious. Once again, just saying thank you isn't good enough. You have to write a proper note in a timely manner for each gift you receive. "Aha," you say, "but isn't that why I'm getting a wife in the first place? So she can take care of things like this?" Nice try, caveboy. Half of those notes are going out to your side of the family and friends, and if you don't want your wife to stab you with a pen, felt-tip or otherwise, you'll contribute more to the process than "Yeah, thanks from me too" on the bottom of each note.

Now that we've determined that writing thank-you notes is something you have to do, how can you make it easier on yourself? One way is to stay current. Make sure you order formal thank-you notes at the same time you order wedding invitations. You'll probably receive several gifts by mail before the wedding day, and if you don't have your notes yet, buy some at a card store to tide you over. Then, instead of just opening prewedding gifts and writing down what they are on the appropriate index card (as discussed in the chapter "Guest List"), get out your thank-you notes and knock them off immediately. One or two a night doesn't seem so bad, and you'll be thankful that some of the heavy writing has already been done when you return from your honeymoon.

When that time comes, however, you will still have a considerable number of notes to write. If the gifts are almost equally divided between your wife's acquaintances and yours, you can each thank the people you know best. If it's unequal, divide it 50/50 anyway, even if it means you have to thank people you've never met.

Unfortunately, since the Big Bird sweater days, you still haven't gotten over the fear of what to write on that blank page. So here's a basic outline to help you create the perfect thank-you note every time.

Dear Mr. and Mrs. Albert and Ludwina Shastakovich,
        Name of guests (double-check spelling!)

Thank you for the lovely *duck-shaped garlic pulverizer.* *Jane Bride*
        Identify gift (assuming you can)   **Your wife**

and I can't wait to have you over for dinner so we can _pulverize the living_

Describe how you plan

hell out of some garlic. It was _just ducky (ha ha ha!)_ to see you at our

to use the gift soon.   **Token gift pun (use sparingly)**

wedding, and we thank you for being such an _inconsequential_ part of our

You're better off lying

big day. _We hope to see you soon._

See, isn't the lie nicer?

Love,

Joe Groom and Jane Bride

There, that was easy, wasn't it?

· *Hers* ·

GIFT RETURN

LET it be said up front that every wedding gift is a treasure. It was selected with care, wrapped with joy, and presented with the best of wishes. Alas, intent does not always equal good taste. In a time when weddings are getting bigger and homes smaller, you simply may not be able to keep and use every wedding gift you receive.

Despite your affection for the givers, if you receive three blenders and not one coffee cup, there's no shame in exchanging goods. In Psych 101, you may have learned about something called Maslow's Hierarchy of Needs, which was a way to categorize all the things human beings need according to how strongly they need them. Similarly, in Weddings 101, we can categorize all the gifts you'll receive into a hierarchy according to how strongly you desire to keep them. For instance, at the top of the pyramid is *money*. People will give you the gift of money in inverse proportion to how much you want it. So cash sits atop the pyramid in terms of desirability, but the actual quantity received is relatively low.

Beneath money is *gifts for which you registered*. Obviously you can buy

anything you want with cold hard cash, but people often dislike the impersonal aspect of writing a check and would prefer to give you something tangible wrapped in silver foil and tied with a bow. Registry gifts satisfy both
giver and receiver.

Next is *gifts for which you didn't register, but are useful anyway*. Almost
anyone can handle an extra vase, salad bowl, or sterling silver picture frame.
Dave and I deliberately didn't register for the ubiquitous chip 'n' dip plate,
thinking we'd never use such a thing. Someone gave us one anyway, and
even though it's covered with engraved glass broccoli spears, I'm not
ashamed to admit we've used it for every party we've thrown since the wedding.

Near the base of the pyramid is *gifts for which you didn't register and can't
possibly use, but are easy to return*. As wedding presents begin to pile up,
you'll develop a keen eye for those that are returnable. Hallmarks of easy-to-
return gifts include:

- boxes or wrapping bearing a store logo

- an enclosed store gift card

- a national brand product

When you start the process of bringing back wedding gifts, you'll quickly
learn that the easiest places to return things are large department stores
with their own bridal registry departments. Whether or not you registered
there, if you go in and politely say, "I received this for my wedding and the
giver thinks she bought it here," the department store will almost always
take back the item, provided they do indeed stock it. They'll either give you
a cash refund (score!) or a store credit. These stores basically have a revolv-
ing-door policy toward their merchandise—it goes out to one bride who
doesn't like it; it comes back; it goes out to another bride; and so on until
someone keeps it.

Let's say you received a garish glass cake plate in a plain tissue-paper-
wrapped box. With no store name or gift card, are you destined to keep the

plate? No! You check for identifying marks on the base and discover that it is made by Mikasa. Your first step is to go to the store where you registered and see if they carry the plate.

If they can't help you, national brands like Mikasa often have their own Mikasa-only stores. You can drop in to one for help, or they probably have a toll-free number where someone can identify the item number of your cake plate through a detailed description and then tell you how you can receive credit for it.

At the very bottom of the pyramid is *gifts for which you didn't register, can't possibly use, and can't return.* This category includes handmade gifts—artwork, pottery, painted porcelain picture frames, cross-stitch samplers of your wedding invitation, embroidered napkins and tablecloths, and crocheted doilies. Also included are various glass and sterling silver items with no identifying brand marks: heart paperweights, candy dishes, salt spoons, and candlesticks, candlesticks, candlesticks. The nice thing about suddenly having four sets of candlesticks is that, should one of your less privileged friends come over, express admiration, and mourn their own candlestickless state, a small gesture on your part can make everyone happy. Ditto the candy dish. Someone you know is dying for a candy dish.

There's a fine line in regifting, however. It's one thing to say, "Gosh, I'm just never going to use this salt cellar and I know you've wanted one ever since fifth grade. Want to borrow mine for a while?" It's something altogether different to rewrap that salt cellar and give it to someone else. You dishonor the original giver; you also wind up looking like the worst kind of cheapskate if you get caught.

Finally, regardless of your personal taste, it's a crime against nature to discard or regift any item that someone has clearly slaved over to create on your behalf. You don't have to hang the needlework sampler on your wall, but you should find a small corner somewhere to store it indefinitely.

·*His*·

GIFT RETURN

MUCH to the chagrin of my new wife, my reaction to every wedding gift we opened was naively optimistic. "Wow! What a great breadmaker!" "Awesome! Look at this fish-shaped cheese board!" "Hey! It's a really nice . . . gift of some sort!" When I was growing up, the only bad gifts were socks and sweaters, and you could usually tell when those were coming because they felt soft through the wrapping paper. After our wedding, I didn't see a single piece of clothing in the pile, just big, hard boxes of glass, ceramic, and metal things and envelopes filled with cash. I was understandably excited by the contents of even the most obscure gift.

My wife took a different approach. Keep the cash, the things we registered for, and the cool unexpected gifts; return duplicates and things that were ugly. But taking back any gift seemed like such a cruel destiny. When I thought of where that unwanted marble dolphin statuette might end up, memories of the Island of Misfit Toys from "Rudolph the Red-Nosed Reindeer" kept popping into my head. Plus, there are those long lines at the returns desk to deal with, rude clerks who want to know why you're returning the gift, and the inevitable collection of store credits you'll amass and never get around to using.

Ever the pragmatist, I decided to make the best of the situation by offering my wife alternative uses for seemingly useless gifts.

- A big ugly bowl makes a great planter.

- What extra cake plates? Oh, you mean our new stained-glass window hangings?

- That third toaster oven holds almost all of my tools!

- This comforter has cats embroidered on it, and Mr. Piddles needs somewhere to sleep. Now, I'm no genius, but I'd say we've got a match.

- Honey, I can't cancel the monthly Hilshire Farms gift subscription. My doctor said specifically that I need to increase my intake of sausage and cheese.

- Who cares what it is? If it can hold pennies, I'll give it a job!

No doubt, these excuses will work about as well for you as they did for me. Which is to say, not at all. My wife returned the unwanted presents or gave them more appropriate homes. "And what will we say," I asked, "if Aunt Jeannie comes to visit and wonders where we've displayed her cubist self-portrait?" The truth—lot B of the city dump—was hardly acceptable. But my wife's solution wasn't much better. "You're the one with all the creative uses for bad gifts," she said. "You come up with an excuse."

Rousted from a male's natural state of laziness, denied my pack-rat sensibilities, mourning the banishment of my misfit gifts, and forced to cover up their abduction, I stood face-to-face with the first real challenge of my marriage. Naturally, I caved. By the time Aunt Jeannie came around looking for her painting, I had my excuse all ready to go. If you find yourself confronted with the dreaded "Where's my gift?" scenario, these all-purpose lies will help you weasel your way out.

- We're having it appraised by Sotheby's.

- It's being dry-cleaned.

- It was stolen by notorious vase (cake plate, dolphin statuette, etc.) thieves.

- Oh, we put it somewhere safe. We're afraid I might . . . um, *some oaf* might accidentally drop it.

- It's far too beautiful for company.

- The question shouldn't be where *is* your gift, but where *isn't* it. Know what I mean?

Or the one I have yet to use, but which may be my personal favorite:

- My wife returned it for cash, which she used to buy booze and chocolate.

· *Hers* ·

CREATING PHOTO ALBUMS

THE fun of wedding photography begins when you choose your photographer, and it climaxes when you have to divide ten thousand shots of you and the groom into permanent albums. You start with a pile of proofs (small three-by-five-inch prints of all the pictures the photographer took). A *big* pile. So big, in fact, that you look at the pile and think, "Can't I just keep one-third, give one-third each to my parents and in-laws, and be done with it?"

Not so fast, missy. First, all the parents will need to see all the proofs, and take dibs on which ones they like. They won't be content with three-by-fives either; they'll want an eight-by-ten glossy of that one at the altar and a couple of five-by-sevens of the garden shots, and come to think of it, they have a six-by-eight frame up in the attic that's crying to be used. The limo picture would do beautifully. Wait a minute—maybe two eight-by-tens and one five-by-seven, and can the photographer airbrush the mole on Uncle Herbert's forehead? Can she crop into circles, or are squares and rectangles the only options?

As your parents make and remake their lists, you'll get sucked into all kinds of interfamilial disputes. Your mother will be upset because she wanted a picture of the two of you without her ex-husband (your father), but in two solid hours of taking pictures, the photographer didn't remember to get that particular shot. And you, amnesiac that you are, didn't remind him. What, were you getting married or something? Your father wants a picture of you with your sister, the maid of honor, but doesn't want all the rest of the bridesmaids involved. "You didn't ask the photographer for that pose? Well, just put on your dress again and have him take it real quick."

Each of your parents will want to put together albums for the grandparents. This gets even more complicated. "You know, Grandma won't really be able to identify that strange young man you're always standing next to in the pictures. Don't we have a bunch of you by yourself we can send her?" By this time they've forgotten that the package you paid a bazillion dollars for was limited to three big albums, four eight-by-ten prints, four six-by-eight prints, and four five-by-seven prints. The cost be damned: they want what they want and all you have to do is sort it out and convey it to the photographer.

None of this takes into account your own feelings. Your fiancé's parents want only those pictures in which the groom looks fabulous and you look like you just swallowed a pound of birdseed. And is there some law of wedding photography that says No Shot Shall Be Perfect? An elbow is awry, or someone is standing funny, or the way you're holding your bouquet makes you look like you have no waist. When you finally find a shot in which everyone seems to look perfect, you notice that the best man was giving bunny ears to the maid of honor.

Finally, it's all done. You give the photographer a master list of everyone's final photographic choices. Then you give him the new, revised list of everyone's final photographic choices. The album arrives—a giant, thirty-pound monstrosity covered in white velveteen. You ooh, you aaah, you fill up all fifteen sterling silver picture frames you received as gifts—and then you never look at any of it again. Who has time to stop and look at wedding pictures when you're so busy being married?

· *His* ·

CREATING PHOTO ALBUMS

HERE'S a story that explains how something as simple as putting photographs in an album can be made into something extraordinarily complicated.

Alan and Cynthia, a couple in the process of coming down from their wedding high, were not overly organized people before their engagement. The demands of planning a wedding in New York for four hundred people, however, had turned them into a highly efficient team. The year before their ceremony was the most active and complicated of their lives, but they rose to meet the challenge, and on the evening of the summer solstice, they pulled off their wedding virtually without a hitch.

At eleven P.M. sharp, amid a shower of birdseed, they piled into a waiting limousine that whisked them off to a hotel near the airport. At seven A.M. the next morning, Alan and Cynthia were on a flight to Greece, where they spent the next two weeks working their way through customs, exchanging money, haggling with street vendors, and enjoying twilight cruises. Upon their return, there were hundreds of thank-you notes to write, a tedious but necessary job, which they polished off in under ten days.

Finally, only one wedding-related task remained: putting together the photo albums. Since they had hired a professional photographer who happened to be a family friend, it would have been easy enough to trust his judgment and leave everything to him. But Alan and Cynthia were still feeling the aftermath of their organizational frenzy, and they both thought that, as their final and most enduring nuptial act, it was essential they micromanage the heck out of the wedding album process.

Step one was to arrange a meeting with each album recipient—three sets of parents and stepparents, and two grandparents, not to mention the bride and groom—to present the proofs and take individual orders for each person's favorite shots. Naturally, nobody picked the same shots, nor were they interested in standard sizes. As for albums, Cynthia's mother was partial to the binder format with the gold leaf, Alan's mother required something Pleather-bound. Some wanted borders, others asked for tissue dividers, and one grandparent insisted that every photo be cropped into the shape of a heart. The order forms Alan was forced to create looked like inventory sheets from Home Depot, but these were the lengths to which he was willing to go to make everyone happy.

Everyone, that is, except the photographer, who took one look at the pile of requests and started to hyperventilate. He asked for two months to deliver the final prints. But Alan's grandmother needed hers the following week because she was going on a cruise, and it was crucial that she show everyone on board the ship what a handsome groom her grandson was. Alan pleaded with the photographer to speed up that particular order. He begged for separate invoices, negotiated specific developing techniques, and sold his soul for custom-made album pages.

The fruits of his labor arrived on-time and within budget. Alan and Cynthia personally delivered each album to its new owner, which, to their surprise, received mixed reviews. "I thought it would be bigger." "I didn't ask for that picture, did I?" "This cost me how much?!!" These were the comments interspersed between the appropriate ooohs and aaaahs. Three years later, neither Alan nor Cynthia has ever removed their album from the bookshelf where they placed it the day they got it. And presumably, the only people who have seen the other albums are the recipients themselves—and the fifteen hundred people on Alan's grandma's cruise ship.

The moral of the story? You, your wife, and your photographer should take one hour and decide which photographs are going to go in the albums. In a month or so, everyone will get the albums you made, and he or she will like them. As for you, when your wedding is over, it's over. Calm down, and go back to being lazy and disorganized like the rest of us.

·*Hers*·

THE HONEYMOON

THE word "honeymoon" has come to be associated with any halcyon period in one's life, not just the traditional trip taken by a bride and groom immediately after their wedding. We speak, for instance, of the honeymoon phase in a new job as those few months when you walk around thinking you have the best boss, co-workers, and career in the whole world. What's usually implicit is that a honeymoon of any kind is temporary: a lull before the inevitable storm hits and you find out that your new office is as packed with petty politics as your last job.

So, is the postwedding trip really just an opportunity for you to gain a false sense of nuptial bliss before the awful reality of married life sets in? Of course not. But the honeymoon can be one of the first tests of your married relationship. Iris, who's been married for twenty years, discovered on her honeymoon how frustrating it is to share one tiny bathroom with a man who kept crowding her when she dressed and undressed and applied and removed her makeup. Add to that the stress of traveling, a touch of postwedding letdown, and the pressure of living up to romantic expectations, and you'll find that a surprising amount of bickering takes place during what is supposed to be the most glorious, fun-packed time of your life.

This is probably why you hear so many honeymoon nightmare stories. One new bride told me about her post-wedding trip to the Bahamas, during which her husband indulged his two great passions: gambling and drinking. By nightfall, he was too tired to do anything but eat dinner and pass out. Another bride was delighted when her fiancé volunteered to plan the honeymoon from start to finish. When he told her it was going to be a camping trip, she pictured a quaint cozy cabin on a lake. But after the wedding, the couple arrived at a shabby little trailer, which they had to enter by breaking in through a window. Since the place was only used two or three times a year as a flophouse for the groom's hunting buddies, there was no heat (in early March), one moldy mattress on the floor, and mouse droppings everywhere.

What these women have in common is that they made the mistake of letting their new husbands make important decisions. When it comes to planning, let's face it, we're the brains of the outfit. Men are fine at being the foot soldiers who execute your orders, but who knows what chaos will ensue when you give them the command deck? To avoid both the risks of ceding responsibility and the burden of organizing a honeymoon in addition to a wedding, what you need to do is set foolproof parameters and let your husband do the actual legwork.

The first item of business is deciding where you're going. For couples who have similar hobbies, likes, and dislikes, the honeymoon destination may be an easy choice. If you're avid skiers or scuba divers, for example, you've probably known since the day you met that you would honeymoon in Vail or Zurich or Belize. But what if you want to go to the beach and he wants to ski? What if you're a wine buff and he couldn't tell a merlot from a cabernet? Differences, after all, are often what draw us to our partner to begin with.

Compromising on a beach location that offers waterskiing might work, or perhaps you could agree to spend one week at the beach and one week at a ski resort. It's a bit more difficult if, for example, you are an adventure traveler while your husband likes to travel in pampered comfort, or if your husband likes to squeeze in a different activity every hour while you like nothing more than a relaxing vacation doing absolutely nothing. Perhaps you're only comfortable traveling with clothing for every possible occasion, while your husband hates checking baggage on a plane and won't travel with more than what he can comfortably carry on.

As with all the issues in your future life together, compromise is the name of the game. Pick a location that offers at least some opportunities to satisfy you both, then turn the task of planning over to your husband. Find a spa in an exotic location that offers adventure *and* pampering. Restrict your travel to a place with one predictable climate so the clotheshorse half of the couple won't feel compelled to pack his or her entire wardrobe. Agree that you don't need to spend every minute together on your honeymoon, and separate so that there are no hard feelings when one of you goes horseback riding while the other takes a nap.

Besides navigating personal and stylistic differences, one of the challenges of a honeymoon is to avoid being intimidated by expectations. Tradition says you're supposed to be swept off your feet on your wedding night, carried effortlessly over the threshold of some impossibly romantic resort, and then made passionate love to until dawn. The reality is more like this: exhausted after hours of revelry capping off months of planning, you and your husband stagger back to the hotel room where you'll crash before hopping on an eight A.M. flight. Your husband gamely suppresses a groan as he carries you over the threshold of room 419 and then sets you down on the bed. You are swept up in a passionate kiss until he unzips your dress and releases the pound of birdseed that has become stuck in your cleavage. Far from having the most meaningful sex of your life, you dissolve into giggles and your spouse retreats to the bathroom.

So what percentage of couples really do have a wedding night filled with fireworks? Well, less than the majority, an informal survey leads me to believe. Leslie and her husband decided to de-stress after their wedding, so they got in the Jacuzzi and became so relaxed they promptly fell asleep. On Pamela's wedding night, she and her husband counted their wedding-gift money and then fell asleep. The next morning, their flight to St. Thomas was delayed six hours. Later in the trip, while on a cruise, Pamela suffered from motion sickness and a terrible cold. When asked about her honeymoon's level of passion, she said, "Put it this way. I had every one of our thank-you notes written and mailed by the time we got home."

· His ·

The Honeymoon

YOUR honeymoon is the chance of a lifetime to go somewhere absolutely amazing and create memories you'll carry with you for the rest of your life. Unfortunately, playing the role of intrepid world traveler requires a great deal of time and energy. Since these resources are never more scarce than during the planning stages of a wedding, many couples skimp on the preliminary planning and find themselves lost on a trip they were ill-prepared to take — or worse, bored out of their minds on an all-inclusive, all-it-took-was-one-phone-call-and-a-big-fat-check-to-plan vacation that takes place on five hundred square yards of fenced-in sand.

Like it or not, a truly memorable honeymoon takes a truckload of advance research. If your budget is tight, it'll take even more work, because you'll have to comparison shop to stretch every dollar to the limit. You may, in fact, have to put just as much effort into planning your honeymoon as you do into planning your wedding. But at the moment when you're hanging up your tux and staring at plane tickets to a country that suddenly seems very foreign, you'll be glad you put in the extra effort.

There are dozens of books that describe travel basics, and your travel agent, parents, or friends who travel frequently will also offer advice. So I'll give you something you can only find here: seven essential tips for turning your honeymoon into a dream vacation that you and your new wife will remember forever.

1. *Tell everyone it's your honeymoon.* This is something Wendy and I learned by accident during our honeymoon in Turkey. We happened to mention at the airport check-in that this was our honeymoon, and within moments we were waiting in the VIP lounge with complementary mini bottles of champagne. After that, believe me, every hotel clerk, waiter, concierge, boat captain, and Turkish delight vendor we encountered knew we were newlyweds. Free wine, free desserts, roses in rooms, complementary serenades, not to mention friendly smiles and misty-eyed congratulations — all these can be yours at the mere mention of two little words: Honey. Moon.

2. *Make love when you want to, not when you should.* Why do you need to have sex on your wedding night? Why can't it wait until you're settled into your honeymoon hotel? And if you're tired from traveling or sightseeing your first day, there's no reason you shouldn't wait until day two to explore the area between the sheets. Putting pressure on yourself to have great sex is like forcing yourself to have a lot of fun. It doesn't work.

3. *Introduce yourselves to other honeymooners.* If you've envisioned a particular destination for your honeymoon, others have probably thought of it too. There's bound to be another friendly couple to talk to on the plane or in your hotel. Use them as dinner companions, on the off chance you and your new wife run out of things to talk about after spending every hour together for three or four straight days (welcome to marriage!). And you can learn from other couples' travel experiences, both positive and negative. Be careful not to let another couple overwhelm you with their presence, though. You may want to draw the line at sharing a room.

4. *Don't skimp on the important things.* Your honeymoon is not the time for bargain travel packages, time-share vacation offers, and second-rate airlines. Spend the extra cash to get the honeymoon suite, the room with an

ocean view, the first class cabin on the cruise ship, the finest wine at a restaurant. If you must save money, go to a top-ranked resort during the off-season, use frequent flier miles to upgrade your airline tickets to first class, and make sure that you buy film and sunblock *before* you leave, so you don't have to pay tourist prices.

5. *Preserve your memories in your heads.* Every couple shoots at least a few rolls of film while they're on their honeymoon. That's to be expected. And a camcorder can capture some nice moments if it's used sparingly. But you don't need to archive every single moment and destination, nor do you have to take a picture of your wife standing in front of every landmark, pointing back at it as if to say, "Look at what I discovered!" The Eiffel Tower was there long before you were, and if you tell your friends and family you saw it, they will believe you. Spend your time enjoying the scenery, not recording it.

6. *Pack half of what you think you'll need.* Especially clothes. Believe it or not, they have laundry service in other states and countries. If worse comes to worst, a rigorous scrub in a bathtub with some shampoo will make everything from underwear to jeans smell like new again. Things you should also leave home: hair dryers, hardcover books, CD collections, pets, laptop computers, favorite pillows, and that ten-pound bag of trail mix you usually travel with.

7. *Your honeymoon belongs to you. Keep it that way.* When you return from your honeymoon in some exotic location, family members may ask what you brought them. The answer should be, abso-bloody-lutely nothing! They can enhance their matchbook, flight napkin, or snow globe collection through some other suckers. *You've* got a honeymoon to enjoy. Forget sending postcards, making long-distance phone calls, and conducting business deals while you're away. No reasonable person expects newlyweds to be thinking about anyone but each other on their honeymoon, and, besides, what are you going to say in a postcard?

"We were having a great time until I had to stop and write this. Glad you're not here. Oh, God, now I have to figure out how much postage to put on this stupid thing. Thanks a lot, jerk. See ya soon!"

THE "I CAN LAUGH ABOUT IT NOW THAT IT'S OVER" GAME

Remember doing Mad Libs as a kid? Well, here's a modified version for adults. It's a fun exercise to tweak the seriousness out of the wedding process and put you back in a good humor once it's all over. During your honeymoon, or when you've returned from it, ask your spouse to provide you with whatever is written in parentheses under each blank. For instance, if a blank asks for an adjective, ask your spouse to say the first adjective that comes to mind. Do *not* read the surrounding story to him or her. Fill in each blank with your spouse's answers. When you've completed all the blanks, read the story out loud and enjoy your wedding from a whole new perspective.

REFLECTIONS ON A WEDDING
(from One Newlywed to Another)

Honey, I can hardly think of anything more _____
(adjective)
than our wedding. I'll never forget the _____, the
(noun)
_____, or the _____ that made the _____
(noun)   (plural noun)   (time of day)
so special. If it wasn't for your _____ breaking
(male relative)
his _____, when he tripped over the _____,
(body part)   (noun)
the whole thing would have been absolutely perfect.

When you _____ me off my feet on the dance floor,
(verb, past tense)

300

I thought I was just going to _____. And when I
(verb)

heard the first notes of _____ I almost lost my
(a song)

_____. You were so _____ and _____ you
(plural noun)   (adjective)   (adjective)

made me feel like the _____est _____ in the
(adjective)   (noun)

world. Now that we're married, there's something I want

you to know. I want _____ kids, so we'd better get
(a number)

_____ right now. No, I'm just kidding. What I
(adjective)

really want to say is, I will always _____ you. And
(verb)

as we grow _____ together, I don't want _____
(adjective)   (noun)

to come between us. Thank you for a truly _____
(adjective)

wedding, and may all our days together be equally

_____.
(adjective)

                                        _____,
                                             (adverb)

                                        _____
                                        (a cute nickname)

301

Afterword

PRESERVING THE MEMORIES: HIS AND HERS

It may seem hard to believe now, but there may come a day when you won't remember much about your wedding or the planning that preceded it. This might be a blessing, as long as you find a way to preserve the best memories and blank out the worst. So we'll wrap up this guide with some suggestions on how to preserve today's events and emotions for tomorrow.

While you're compiling photo albums for your parents and yourselves, don't forget to pick a few favorite shots to be framed. Give them a prominent place in your home, on a mantel or a shelf near the front door. And take one picture to work so that colleagues can exclaim over the wedding dress. When you're having a bad day, a framed wedding photo is an instant reminder of one of the happiest moments of your life.

If you've never kept a diary or a journal, the period before your wedding would be a great time to start. Nothing captures your feelings and motivations during this exciting time of your life quite like your own words on paper. Keeping a daily record of events forces you to record the tiniest occurrences, things that you'd probably forget over time but may be worth a few minutes of reminiscence years down the line.

You can also turn your journal into a scrapbook, or turn the scrapbook into a shoebox filled with wedding knickknacks: an invitation, a party favor, cuff links, wedding earrings, a sachet of birdseed, a dried flower from the bouquet, pictures from the rehearsal dinner, the ring bearer's pillow, plane tickets and a champagne cork from the honeymoon, and the figurines from the top of your wedding cake. Keep these trinkets hidden away until some special occasion, like your third anniversary or seventh Valentine's Day together. Then dust off the box and go through the memories together.

A Saturday morning will soon arrive with no phone calls to make, no restaurants to inspect, and no people to please. Your thank-you note file will be complete and sitting in its permanent resting place on the back of some closet shelf. You'll read the paper, run some errands, share a meal, go about your day. And the two of you will realize that this is what it's like to be husband and wife.

After coming through a time of great upheaval, manic activity, and vivid emotions, many people find themselves asking, "What's next? Should I just wait and see what happens, or is there something else I can work on?" Well, there is another project in front of you, perhaps the most important one of all. That project is your marriage, and while the perspectives of married life will always be divided into "His" and "Hers," your ongoing job will be converting them peacefully into "Ours." The skills you've developed while planning your wedding will help you achieve this goal.

The difference between working on your wedding and working on your marriage is the difference between trying to get somewhere and enjoying the ride. Your energies may be currently focused on the success of a one-day event. But the long-term success of your marriage is a lifelong effort, a series of opportunities to strengthen teamwork, build respect, and deepen love between a man and a woman. From your first anniversary through your fifty-fifth, there are years of funny stories yet to come, and many more challenges to survive together.

For now, just know that you will, at the very least, survive your wedding. What's more, we hope you now have the perspective and some good advice to help you go beyond survival toward enjoyment. We wish you the happiest of all possible weddings from both his and her points of view, and a marriage that thrives on a healthy balance of both.